AGA

The Story of a Kitchen Classic

'Some years ago, when outfitting my new villa,
I had cause to look into the economy and
efficiency of modern types of kitchen ranges.
It seemed to me that a stove could be made
that was more in tune with the high demands
and the development of the technique of our time.
I have tried to solve the problem and
have now constructed a kitchen range
which I think meets rather exacting demands
on convenience and low running costs…'

Dr Gustaf Dalén

inventor of the Aga, speaking in 1922

The Story of a Kitchen Classic

Tim James

Absolute Press

First published in Great Britain in 2002 by
Absolute Press
Scarborough House
29 James Street West
Bath BA1 2BT
England
Phone 44 (0) 1225 316013
Fax 44 (0) 1225 445836
E-mail info@absolutepress.demon.co.uk
Web www.absolutepress.demon.co.uk

A catalogue record of this book is available from the
British Library

ISBN 1 899791 54 X

Printed and bound by Butler & Tanner, Frome, Somerset

For Laura with love and thanks

Contents

BESKRIVNING

OFFENTLIGGJORD AV

KUNGL. PATENT- OCH REGISTRERINGSVERKET.

SVENSKA AKTIEBOLAGET GASACCUMULATOR,

STOCKHOLM.

Kokspis med värmeackumulator.

(Uppfinnare: G. Dalén.)

Klass 36: a.

Patent i Sverige från den 3 oktober 1922.

Föreliggande uppfinning avser en kokspis med värmeackumulator av metall och kännetecknas därigenom, att värmeackumulatorn är kombinerad med en för kontinuerlig förbränning avsedd magasinseldstad för fast bränsle, så att den uppsamlar värmet från denna eldstad, för att vid behov d. v. s. då kokning skall äga rum, avgiva det ackumulerade värmet till kokkärlen eventuellt under automatisk ökning av fyren. Den nämnda eldstaden kan matas med bränsle från ett bränslemagasin, som kan vara anbragt inuti den av ett metallblock utförda värmeackumulatorn, eller också kan det-

avtagande temperaturer. Sådana värmeackumulatorer med lägre temperatur kunna utgöra av en eller flera stekugnar samt en eller flera s. k. koklådor.

Bifogade ritning visar såsom exempel olika utföringsformer av uppfinningen. Fig. 1 visar en kokspis i vertikal genomskärning, försedd med en enda värmeackumulator, under det att fig 2 visar, ävenledes i vertikalgenomskärning men i mindre skala, en kokspis med flera värmeackumulatorer. resp. med stekugn och koklåda. Fig. 3 och 4 visa andra utförings-former.

Preface

It is tempting to speculate on what Dr Gustaf Dalén, the Swedish Nobel Laureate who invented the Aga in 1922, would have made of the success his creation has gone on to achieve. Blinded in an horrific accident, Dalén could be subject to dramatic mood swings. He once asked: 'What do they expect of me who can no longer do anything?' Yet he was also respected by his peers and staff for his stoicism. He clocked in every day at his factory on Lidingö island and presented every member of his workforce with a lapel badge bearing, in Swedish, the slogan *'Be optimistic'*.

Such faith was well placed. Today, 80 years on, the Aga born of Dalén's creative vision is acknowledged as an impressive feat of engineering and a design classic. More significantly, the Aga has come to occupy a unique place in the hearts and minds of its owners. Few products attract such enthusiasm and loyalty.

Put at its simplest, the Aga is special. While having continually undergone development, the Aga today is essentially the same cooker as that built in Dalén's kitchen at home just four years after the end of the First World War. The Aga, with its stubborn resistance to the electronic gimmickry of the modern kitchen, has sustained an enduring appeal which has defied the fickle finger of fashion. The Aga has a strand of popular English literature named after it. It has remained the cooker of choice of the rich and famous – from Queen Mary in the 1930s to Jamie Oliver in 2002. It continues to be as much a part of country living as green wellingtons and early closing on Wednesdays; and, as it celebrates its eightieth birthday, the Aga is today attracting the attentions of a younger and more metropolitan audience.

This is the story of the Aga through the memories of those who know it best: friends and family of Dr Dalén; Aga owners, distributors, engineers and staff; those who cast its legend in iron; those who helped develop it from solid-fuel range to modern lifestyle icon; and those charged with taking it forward in a new millennium.

I owe a debt of gratitude to all those who helped by sharing with me their reminscences and their expertise. I hope you enjoy reading *their* story of the Aga as much as I enjoyed writing it.

TIM JAMES

1869-1929

The vision of a genius

'Some years ago, when outfitting my new villa, I had cause to look into the economy and efficiency of modern types of kitchen ranges. I have tried to solve the problem and have now constructed a kitchen range which I think meets rather exacting demands on convenience and low running costs…'
Dr Gustaf Dalén

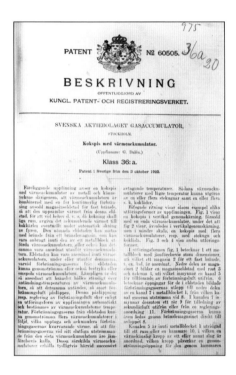

Dr Gustaf Dalén patented his invention in Sweden on 3 October 1922

How right he proved to be. Dr Gustaf Dalén, a renowned Swedish physicist and Nobel Prize winner, had invented what was to become the internationally renowned Aga. It was a project he cared about deeply: he believed that he was striving to create an 'invention for ordinary people'.

Today, more than eight decades later, the range cookers spawned by his genius are at the heart of more than 750,000 homes around the world. Dalén's invention transformed kitchen life… and he never got to see it.

For the Aga was born out of tragedy. In 1912, 10 years before the launch of his revolutionary new cooker, Dalén was badly injured when an experiment went horribly wrong. Though he slowly recovered from his other injuries, Dalén

permanently lost sight in both eyes.

Whilst convalescing at home after his accident Dalén realised the difficulties his wife, Elma, had cooking on her traditional kitchen range. It needed constant attention, devoured vast amounts of fuel and was, by his exacting standards, poorly designed. It was logical to Dalén that he should apply his scientific thinking to the design of a cooker.

Confined to darkness and forced to rely on his wife to be his eyes, he struggled to give shape to his vision of how much better a range cooker could be, often working long into the night.

He patented the Aga in 1922 and, in 1929, it was launched in Britain to immediate acclaim. In his blindness, Dr Gustaf Dalén had developed and eventually perfected the world's first heat-storage stove.

Dalén photographed in 1895 during his university years in Gothenburg. He graduated as an engineer in 1896, but felt compelled, initially, to help his father with chores on the family farm

Writing in a 1933 British promotional brochure for the Aga, W. T. Wren, Managing Director of the UK distributors of the new Aga, was enthusiastic about the virtues of the new product his sales teams were busy selling into kitchens the length of the land.

'Owners, you will find, come to talk about and regard their Aga as though it were almost another member of the household – a fond personality which has won their affections. Servants love it. So do I…'

Early consumer reaction to the interesting new stove was positive. M. Gibson Watt, of Rhayader, Radnorshire, wrote to Bell's Heat Appliances, of Slough – 'Sole Licensees and Manufacturers for the British Empire (except Canada)' – to praise the new Aga's versatility and reliability.

'I should like to tell you that I find the Aga does all that you claim for it and a good deal more,' he wrote. 'This week we have in the house: 12 in [sic] dining room, 9 servants, 3 in nursery, and besides all this, involving separate meals, we had a dance in the house for 130 people, the supper for which was entirely done at home.'

Another correspondent, Mrs E. M. Evans, of Kensington, London, added her plaudits. She wrote: 'I am very pleased with my Aga. I can assure you that we cannot praise the Aga enough and it may interest you to know that even my housemaid, when talking of it yesterday, said it had quite revolutionised cooking.'

And T. W. Hartley, an industrial engineer from Seisdon near Wolverhampton, contacted Bell's Heat Appliances to praise his new Aga: 'I want to take this opportunity of saying how delighted we are with the stove,' he wrote. 'Your advertisements understate its advantages. My wife states it is one of the best investments we have ever made…'

Amazingly it is not for the Aga that Gustaf Dalén is most widely recognised. It is as the father of an invention that improved safety levels at sea immeasurably, saving literally thousands of lives over many decades.

Dalén was known to his contemporaries in Sweden as the

Dalén's invention of automatic valves for lighthouses was sorely needed. According to lighthouse historian D. Alan Stevenson, in 1833 the average number of ships being wrecked annually on British shores alone was 800. More lighthouses improved matters, as did the installation over the years of better lanterns.

But lighthouses were expensive to maintain and unreliable – savage, unforgiving storms, their very inaccessibility and even absentee keepers could wreak fatal havoc.

The desperate situation was often made worse by the infamous 'moon cussers' – villains who would set up false lights to lure ships on to rocks, only to plunder them when they had run aground. Survivors were often killed; the 'moon cussers' (so called because their dastardly plans would fail under the glare of a bright moon) wanted no witnesses to their violent piracy.

Reliable lighthouses changed all this. Thousands of seafarers would come to thank Dalén for saving their lives through his invention of the Solventil, a valve which allowed a beacon to light automatically at dusk and extinguish itself at dawn. The device, for which Dalén became famous around the globe, enabled lighthouses to function perfectly and be left unattended for periods of up to a year.

'Benefactor to Sailors' for his work on an ingenious device which enabled the lanterns in lighthouses and warning buoys to be switched on and off automatically. This was the Solventil, a valve which allowed a beacon to light automatically at dusk and extinguish itself at dawn.

The invention transformed travel by sea – not only in the treacherous waters around the Swedish coastline with its numerous reefs and archipelagos, but around the globe. It was for this 'gift to humanity' that the Royal Swedish Academy of Sciences voted to award him the 1912 Nobel Prize for Physics. Its President described Dalén's invention as 'an entirely new standard of safety in navigation and an enormous economy'.

The Father of the Aga

Nils Gustaf Dalén was born in Stenstorp in Skaraborg, a province of Vastergötland in southern Sweden, on November 30, 1869, the son of a peasant farmer. Although he is said to have detested farm chores, the young Dalén's flair for invention first shone in his early days on the farm, when he built a threshing machine powered by an old spinning wheel with which he shelled the winter's supply of dried beans.

According to his biographer, Erik Wästberg (1905-1954), Dalén's second invention was yet more fantastic: a 'sleep-prolonger'. In an essay written for *Science News Letter* and later published in condensed form in *Readers Digest*, Wästberg described the young boy's flair for mechanics.

'All his life Dalén hated to get up in the morning, insisted [sic] on nine hours' sleep each night. He rigged an old clock to rotate a spool at a set time. The spool ignited a match which, by an elaborate arrangement of cords and levers, in turn lighted an oil lamp. A coffee pot hug over the lamp flame. In 15 minutes the clock started a hammer beating against an iron plate – and Gustaf was awakened in a lighted room, with hot coffee ready.'

After completing his preliminary education, Gustaf Dalén entered agricultural school to study dairy farming. But he was advised by a mentor who recognised his natural

As a child, Dalén invented a so-called Sleep-Prolonger to maximise his time in bed

gift for mechanics that he should concentrate on seeking a technical education. While still in his teens, Dalén invented a milk tester, which he took to Stockholm to show off to Gustaf de Laval, inventor of a device to separate cream. 'What a coincidence,' said de Laval, according to Wästberg. He then unveiled his own plans for an identical device, for which he had already secured a patent.

Wästberg continues: 'Young Dalén promptly asked for a job in de Laval's laboratory. "Not yet," the older man replied. "Get a sound education first".'

Dalén was keen to make his mark within the engineering community, but more mundane pressures forced him to be patient. With his elder brothers already working in the wider world, Dalén was required by his father to stay at home to help maintain the family farm.

He did as he was requested and, during this time, met and fell in love with the 15-year-old girl he was later to marry.

'I will not be a farmer's wife,' Elma Persson told him, and he did

not want to be a farmer. By the age of 23, Dalén was able to move on. He followed de Laval's advice and gained admission to the prestigious Chalmers Institute in Gothenburg in 1892. He graduated as an engineer four years later. After graduation, he spent a year in Switzerland, studying at the Eidgenössisches Polytechnikum, before he was finally ready to take up the promised appointment in the de Laval works in Stockholm. He was also ready – and better placed – to marry the girl who had waited for him with such devotion. Gustaf and Elma moved into a flat in Stockholm where, says Wästberg, Dalén spent 'every free moment on his experiments'.

Dalén became Technical Chief of the Svenska Karbid-och Acetylen A.B. [Swedish Carbide and Acetylene Ltd.] in 1901 and later joined the Gas Accumulator Company, where he became Chief Engineer in 1906. It was this company which was to be the first to bear the Aga name: in 1909, the firm was reorganised as Svenska Aktiebolaget Gasaccumulator (AGA) [Swedish Gas Accumulator

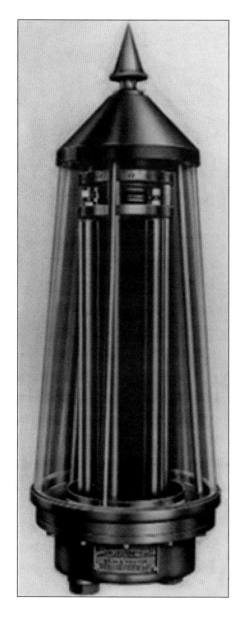

Above: Dalén's patented Solventil revolutionised lighthouse technology

Opposite page: the AGA factory on Lidingö island

Ltd.] with Dalén himself as Managing Director.

The factory in Stockholm began as a simple workshop and acetylene filling plant employing 16 staff. Today, with only the middle section of the original building remaining, the Swedish AGA company has headquarters on Lidingö island, on the outskirts of the city, and is still one of the world's premier gas companies.

In 1901, the year Dalén married Elma Persson, his company purchased the patent rights to the French invention of dissolved acetylene. Acetylene dissolved in acetone is non-explosive, but as the solution is used explosive gas accumulates in the space left above the liquid.

Dalén developed a porous substance which he called 'aga', and which he enclosed in a small steel container. He filled the container halfway with acetone and added acetylene under pressure, compressing the gas so that the container held 100 times as much acetylene as it would under normal pressure.

The aga remained in place as the solution was used, and, as a consequence, no spaces developed. Dalén had invented the gas accumulator, meaning that, for the first time, acetylene could be handled without risk of detonation from jolting.

The invention led directly to the automatic switch for lighthouse lanterns which Dalén was to call the Solventil. Simply put, he had built on the science behind the wearing of light-coloured clothes in hot weather, the better to reflect the sun's rays. The device had four metal rods suspended vertically inside a glass cylinder. Three of the rods were highly polished and surrounded the fourth, blackened and mounted in the centre of the cylinder.

Sunlight reflecting from the brighter rods warmed the black rod, which expanded and pressed a lever that closed a gas valve, extinguishing the flame. When sunlight faded, the central rod cooled and contracted, the valve opened and the gas was ignited by a small, constantly lit flame called a bypass jet, or pilot light. By raising or lowering the four rods,

Shortly before the accident which cost him his sight, Dalén told two visiting American engineers keen to see his work first hand that he was confident the experiment was entirely safe. 'It is not at all dangerous,' he told them...

Opposite page: minutes before disaster... Dalén (with cane) and his assistants test the safety of an acetylene cylinder by hanging it over an open fire. As they approached the fire for closer inspection the cylinder exploded, seriously injuring Dalén and leaving him blind

the Solventil could be set to open at any degree of darkness.

Not all were convinced, however. According to Erik Wästberg, when Thomas Edison learned of Dalén's invention he simply said, 'It won't work.' The German Patent Office dismissed the idea as 'impossible'.

It did work, however, and when Dalén's invention was unveiled to the world it received widespread acclaim.

The Solventil succeeded in conserving gas and allowing lighthouses and beacons to operate unattended for months at a time. Even after many of the gaslit navigational lights had been converted to electricity, the Solventil was still used in more remote locations.

One of the earliest AGA lighthouses was the Blockhusudden installation off Lidingö island, where the lantern operated – without interruption – from 1912 until its electrification in 1980. Visible from the AGA company's offices on the island, it served as a beacon to Dalén's genius, flashing, it has been estimated, some 400 million times in those 68 years.

'It is not at all dangerous...'

In 1912, however, as the scientific community in Sweden and farther afield was learning of Dalén's invention, tragedy struck in a quarry in Alby near the town of Botkyrka.

Dalén and Elma had just moved into a handsome villa overlooking Stockholm's harbour when two American engineers visited, hoping to discuss problems of safety with the now well-known Swedish inventor. The visitors were interested in understanding how Dalén's acetylene accumulators would react in the case of fire. Dalén told them: 'It is not at all dangerous.'

Encouraged by this confidence, the group lit a large fire in a nearby quarry face and hung gas-filled cylinders over it. At first, the safety devices built into the cylinders worked perfectly. On the fifth iteration of the experiment, however, those observing noticed the gas pressure was falling. Dalén and two of his staff waited a full half an hour before approaching the fading fire. It was then that one of the steel cylinders exploded 'with a

Opposite page: despite now being blind, Gustaf Dalén clocked in at work every day at the AGA factory in Stockholm

Below: in a bizarre twist of fate, Albin Dalén, a respected Swedish eye surgeon, volunteered to operate on his brother in a vain attempt to save his sight

report that was heard for miles'.

'By a miracle, the two assistants escaped with only minor injuries,' writes Wästberg, 'but Dalén was covered by the scalding mass and one of his eyes was almost torn from its socket.

'Rescuers beat the fire from his burning clothing with their bare hands. Dalén's first words were to ask if others had been hurt. When told they were not injured seriously, he said: "I am glad. It is only right that I, who am responsible, should suffer most."'

Doctors initially feared the great Swedish scientist would lose his life, but his strong peasant body fought back. His sight, however, was gone. He was to be blind for the rest of his life.

Dalén was too unwell to travel to the Royal Academy for the presentation of the 1912 Nobel Prize for Physics. In his presentation speech, however, Professor H. G. Söderbaum, the Academy's President, left the assembled audience of royalty, academics and journalists in no doubt as to the importance of his work:

Your Majesty, your Royal Highnesses, ladies and gentlemen, The Royal Academy of Sciences believes it is acting in strict accordance with Alfred Nobel's will in awarding the Physics Prize to Chief Engineer Gustaf Dalén in recognition of his remarkable invention of automatic valves designed to be used in combination with gas accumulators in lighthouses and lightbuoys.

The use of aga light facilitates the placing of lighthouses and lightbuoys in the most inaccessible places… With the use of one or more of the easily transportable gas accumulators, such lights can give their warning or guiding signals for a whole year or more without the need of inspection or the fear of failure.

The result is an entirely new standard of safety in navigation and an enormous economy. For example, one shoal in Swedish waters previously required a lightship

The award of the 1912 Nobel Prize saddened Dalén, who is said to have replied: 'What do they expect of me who can no longer do anything!'

Should the Nobel Prize have gone to Einstein?

At the time of the presentation of the 1912 Nobel Prize to Dalén some academics argued it should instead have been made to Albert Einstein and the Dutch mathematician, Hendrik Antoon Lorentz, for their early work on the Theory of Relativity. Though Lorentz received the 1902 prize for his mathematical theory of the electron and Einstein would receive the 1921 Prize for his services to Theoretical Physics, no one was ever awarded a Nobel Prize for the special or general theories of relativity, one of mankind's greatest discoveries.

costing approximately 200,000 kronor and maintained at a cost of about 25,000 kronor a year. Now, in many cases, navigation is adequately served by establishing an aga buoy with optical and audio signalling apparatus, the cost of which is 9,000 kronor, and the annual maintenance of which costs about 60 kronor.

The annual benefit to navigation can be expressed in terms of saving of thousands of human lives and of hundreds of millions of kronor. The aga flame has proved to be extremely useful in other fields, such as the lighting of railway coaches, railway signalling apparatus, car head-lights, soldering, the casting and cutting of metals and so on. The Academy of Sciences recognises the true value of all these applications and wishes to emphasise those which contribute to the progress of navigation, because it is uncontestably these that have rendered the greatest benefit to humanity.

With that, Professor Söderbaum presented the Nobel medal and diploma to Dalén's brother, Professor Albin Dalén, then of the Caroline Institute. In doing so, he added: 'Professor, when handing over to your brother the medal and the diploma, I beg you also to convey to him from the Royal Academy of Sciences, our sincere congratulations on the distinction he has merited, and our best wishes for a complete and speedy recovery.'

The award of the 1912 Nobel Prize, though, saddened Dalén, who is said to have replied: 'What do they expect of me who can no longer do anything!' His gold Nobel medal is today stored in a Swedish bank vault.

However, the Benefactor to Sailors (as he was known) continued to build on his scientific reputation. Amongst the many distinctions conferred upon him were membership of the Swedish Royal Academy of Sciences in 1913, and of the Academy of Science and Engineering six years later. He was made Honorary Doctor of Lund University in 1918 and received the

Dalén's reputation spread far and wide. In 1932, two royal brothers – both later to become kings of England – visited the AGA factory. Dalén (centre) and his son, Gunnar, (far right) are pictured welcoming George, Duke of York (back to camera) and Edward, Prince of Wales

Above: a contemporary poster advertising the AGA car, the Thulin

Below: the AGA incubator

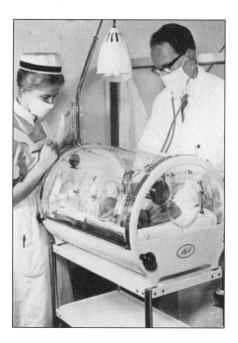

Morehead Medal of the International Acetylene Association. He took part in debates at the National Society of Economics and for almost 20 years served his local community as a member of Lidingö City Council.

Dalén refused to allow his blindness to hamper his work as a scientist and businessman. He soldiered on with his research and his company went from strength to strength. The firm had been awarded the high-profile contract to provide lighting for the Panama Canal and by 1915 there were AGA companies in seven countries. Fuelled by wartime demand for acetylene for beacons, by 1928 subsidiary companies had been formed in a further 17 European and Latin American countries.

Indeed the group was to be behind some of the twentieth century's best-known developments. The AGA car – the Thulin (described in an advertisement at the time to be a 'giant in performance, a dwarf in consumption') was manufactured in Sweden under licence from German AGA. In 1928, AGA formed a separate company, Svenska Radio AB, in conjunction with ASEA and LM Ericsson, the now internationally known telecommunications group. The consortium manufactured the AGA Radio, Europe's first mains-powered wireless.

By 1939 the AGA incubator was being used in hospitals for the care of premature babies. In 1954 the company introduced the world's first heart-lung machine and, in 1952, AGA demonstrated its own colour television.

Then, in 1969, AGA perhaps reached its inventive high point when the NASA astronaut Neil Armstrong installed on the surface of the moon a laser reflector made by the AGA-owned Boxton-Beel company.

But all this lay in the future. In his speech at the 1912 Nobel Prize ceremony the President of the Royal Swedish Academy hinted at the work which was to have greatest impact on kitchens in Great Britain and around the world. He told the assembled dignitaries that

*Top: Dalén's home,
Villa Eckbacken, on
Lidingö island*

*Bottom: (l-r): Dalén's
daughter-in-law Margareta
Uggla, his grandson,
Gustaf Silfverstolpe
and the Daléns' maid,
Anna-Karin Andersson*

Dr Gustaf Dalén had 'turned to the field of thermal technics to invent a stove…which maintains cooking heat for 24 hours using only eight pounds of coal'.

The vision takes shape

Much of the testing of the prototype Aga cooker took place in Dalén's own home, Villa Eckbacken, on Lidingö island during the 1920s. (Since 1968, his home has been the official residence of the Canadian Ambassador and features a number of frescoes, including lighthouses and, in Dalén's study, motifs of the revolutionary Solventil device.)

Anna-Karin Andersson, the Daléns' maid at Villa Eckbacken, recalls how the scientist refused to allow blindness to handicap him in his work.

'Gustaf worked on the Aga cooker in his spare time and I remember going into the kitchen one night and finding him standing on top of the Aga in the dark conducting one of his experiments! I also remember that, at one time, there were two Aga cookers in the kitchen as one was an experimental

oil Aga which remained in the kitchen until 1941.'

Dalén's daughter, Inga-Lisa, recalls life at Villa Eckbacken being somewhat chaotic. She had particular sympathy for the family cook, Anna Lindberg, 'for all the trouble she had to face when different prototypes of cookers went in and out of the kitchen accompanied by workers from the nearby AGA factory'.

The inventor's grandson, Gustaf Silverstolpe, is proud of the legacy left him. 'All my life,' he said, 'Dr Gustaf Dalén – Papa – has been in my memory. He was outstanding in so many ways. He never complained about his blindness – he lived as though he could see.'

Silverstolpe recalls family stories of how Dalén – immortalised in the Swedish classic film *Seger i Mörter* (*Victory in Darkness*) directed by Olof Bergstrom in 1954 – took the trouble to memorise where friends and relations would be seated at the dinner table so he might turn his head to address them, thereby putting them at ease. 'He would

have been very proud of what is being done with the Aga, his invention, after so many years.'

In 1936, the 67-year-old President of AGA attended a company board meeting. 'My doctor tells me,' he told the assembled executives, 'that I have a cancer which cannot be cured. I shall go on as long as possible.' He then insisted on moving on to the next item of business on the agenda.

Nils Gustaf Dalén died on December 9, 1937, at his villa on Lidingö island overlooking the harbour. As ships from around the world made their way through the channel, each reduced its rate of knots and lowered its flags as a mark of respect for the man whose invention, 25 years before, had made the seas a safer place...

Left and right: Dalén at home with his wife Elma

Following pages: Dalén's funeral at Engelbrekt's Church in Stockholm, on 17 December 1937

'On 17th December 1937, while a whirling snowstorm swept over the city of Stockholm, the remains of Dr Dalén were taken to their final resting place. The stormy weather and the falling dusk made one's thoughts wander from the illuminated church – where a large assembly were preparing to bid farewell to the man who had created light for the safety of his fellow men – out to the rocks and the sea and to foreign coasts where in weather like this the unfailing beacons, achieved through his inventive power, were most needed. The storm seemed to summon us to make the reflection that Gustaf Dalén was dead, but that his work would live...'

Eulogy to Dr Dalén in a commemorative edition of the AGA Journal

The Aga arrives in Britain

The Aga first came to the UK in 1929, when it was marketed under licence from AGA in Sweden by Bell's Asbestos and Engineering Supplies Ltd, based at the Bestobell Works in Slough, at that time still part of Buckinghamshire. The journey from continental Europe was not, however, a smooth one. Despite an international reputation, Bell's had to work hard to woo the Aga's Swedish owners.

An internal memorandum sent in 1929 to key directors within Bell's hints at the care Dr Dalén's Gas Accumulator Company took in finding the right partner overseas.

Following the preliminary conversation with Mr Von Heidenstam [later to become Managing Director of Swedish AGA] it would appear that in order to ensure the successful introduction of their patent stove to the British markets, Aga require:-
1. Manufacturing facilities;
2. Specialist selling organisations.
The Aga stove ought, in our opinion, to be introduced as a revolution in household fuel economy – the first seriously insulated cooking medium offered to the British public. If so, presented by Bell's Asbestos, whose reputation in the British insulating world is of long standing and whose selling organisation in the United Kingdom... is probably the only comprehensive one of its kind... for the small user through the medium of its own technical salesmen (over 50 in the United Kingdom), Aga would not only be assured of an immediate and natural entrée to the right quarters, but also of intelligent spade work capable of development on intensive lines as and when the public response justified it.
In conclusion, we are ready to demonstrate our confidence in our own ability to achieve the desired results.

In turn, the Gas Accumulator Company, through its offices in Brentford, did its own homework on the proposed UK partner. According to files lodged at Somerset House, Sweden was told that 'the company was incorporated 1st January 1929 with a nominal capital of £25,000, of which

Above: Aga Sweden's UK Gas Accumulator Company offices in Brentford, Middlesex.

Below: the 'managers and representatives conference' at the Bestobell Works in Slough, October 3 1930

£5,000 has been issued'.

Checks were made with the Midland Bank as to 'whether it would be safe to give credit to that company for £5,000 to £10,000'. The bank replied that it would 'be good for the smaller amount'!

Importantly for Aga Sweden, the new firm was associated with Bell's United Asbestos Ltd, which had 'an issued capital of £1,004,500' and the conclusion passed to the board of the Gas Accumulator Company on Lidingö island in Stockholm was that 'the reference is favourable'.

Soon after the deal was struck a separate company, Bell's Heat Appliances Ltd, was established to market the new breed of cooker to the great British public. Manufacturing itself began in Brentford in 1932 and, in 1936, it was taken over by Aga Heat Ltd, owned by Allied Ironfounders Ltd, a powerful consortium of leading British iron foundries. Aga Heat Ltd was based at Orchard House, Orchard Street, London W1 – boasting a Mayfair phone number and dedicated showrooms at 20 North Audley Street in the West End, 'just opposite Selfridge's'.

It was this company which was to spearhead the campaign to sell the Aga to British royalty, gentry, home-owners, housewives and cooks to such effect that, by the late 1940s, more than 50,000 Aga cookers had been installed.

The making of a classic

That the Aga today is acknowledged as a design classic owes much to the fact that its essential features – both technical and aesthetic – have changed little over the eight decades since it was first patented. While significant improvements have, of course,

been made, the Aga introduced to British consumers in 1929 was remarkably similar to those on sale today. Then, behind the so-called ash-room door – which had always to be kept closed – the Aga burned coke or anthracite within a grate. A thermostatic valve regulated the amount of air required for efficient combustion by automatically closing when the cooker became too hot and opening again when required. A separate valve allowed the user to modify somewhat the running temperature.

The combustion gases, when passing to the chimney, transmitted their heat to the accumulating iron masses which, in turn, were connected to the hotplates and the two ovens.

The Aga had two hotplates; for the 1930s maid, or housewife keen to keep her husband's shirts crisp, these also allowed for flat irons to be heated quickly and efficiently.

The cooker was sold to concerned housewives and maids as being safe to work with. A 1933 brochure read: 'No outside part of the Aga ever gets hot enough to hurt you. The Aga is safe for children, as well as grown-ups.'

The early Agas included a hot water tank built into the cooker. This held around 40 litres, with a tap fitted to the front panel. A drain cock was also fitted, with replenishing of cold water either carried out by hand or by connecting the tank to the household water supply.

Interestingly, while early models were available in the UK only with cream enamelling, the very first models featured a black top and white front panels. The hotplate covers were polished and all fittings were nickel-plated.

Aga in Sweden was proud of its export. The June 1930 edition of the *Aga Journal* – 'House organ for Gasaccumulator' – summarises the product's appeal...

'In the construction of the Aga cooker, aesthetic and hygienic requirements have been most carefully studied. The Aga cooker may be said to fulfil all the reasonable requirements that may be expected from a modern kitchen range.'

The introduction of the Aga to Britain was to prove an enormous challenge for, firstly, Bell's Engineering & Asbestos Ltd, and then the ambitious Bell's Heat Appliances Ltd, sole licensees and manufacturers in the UK.

Early sales figures were very encouraging. The company sold 322 new Agas during 1931 and in 1932 this figure rose to a staggering 1,705. But the firm was experiencing recurring problems with the barrels within which the fuel was burned. The cost of replacements ate into profits and, by September 1933, Aga in Sweden was being informed by its representatives in Britain that 'it would appear that a profit of some £18,000 has been turned into a loss of £9,000, the cause of which is common to all concerned. The monetary situation is becoming acute and, of course, the present state of affairs [a worldwide slump] does not lend itself towards obtaining fresh outside capital...The Bank's and

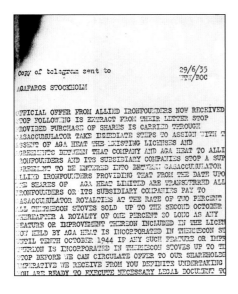

Copy of telegram sent to   29/6/35
            AGAFAROS STOCKHOLM   WTW/POC

OFFICIAL OFFER FROM ALLIED IRONFOUNDERS NOW RECEIVED
STOP FOLLOWING IS EXTRACT FROM THEIR LETTER STOP
PROVIDED PURCHASE OF SHARES IS CARRIED THROUGH
GASACCUMULATOR TAKE IMMEDIATE STEPS TO ASSIGN WITH T
ASSENT OF AGA HEAT THE EXISTING LICENSES AND
AGREEMENTS BETWEEN THAT COMPANY AND AGA HEAT TO ALLI
IRONFOUNDERS AND ITS SUBSIDIARY COMPANIES STOP A SUP
AGREEMENT TO BE ENTERED INTO BETWEEN GASACCUMULATOR
ALLIED IRONFOUNDERS PROVIDING THAT FROM THE DATE UPO
THE SHARES OF   AGA HEAT LIMITED ARE TRANSFERRED ALLI
IRONFOUNDERS OR ITS SUBSIDIARY COMPANIES PAY TO
GASACCUMULATOR ROYALTIES AT THE RATE OF TWO PERCENT
ALL THERMECON STOVES SOLD UP TO THE SECOND OCTOBER
HEREAFTER A ROYALTY OF ONE PERCENT SO LONG AS ANY
FEATURE OR IMPROVEMENT THEREON INCLUDED IN THE LICEN
NOW HELD BY AGA HEAT IS INCORPORATED IN THERMECON ST
UNTIL TENTH OCTOBER 1944 IF ANY SUCH FEATURE OR IMPR
THEREON IS INCORPORATED IN THERMECON STOVES UP TO TH
STOP BEFORE WE CAN CIRCULATE OFFER TO OUR SHAREHOLDE
IMPERATIVE WE RECEIVE FROM YOU DEFINITE UNDERTAKING
YOU ARE READY TO EXECUTE NECESSARY LEGAL DOCUMENT TO

Above: an extract from a telegram sent in June 1935 alerting AGA Sweden to the official offer from the British company Allied Ironfounders Ltd

Opposite page: an Aga advertisement from 1935

Following pages: 1930s advertising images for the Aga promoted the cooker as a boon for housewife and maid alike

Bell's other resources are, I understand, rather dried up.'

The solution was the acquisition in 1934 by the newly established Aga Heat Ltd of the interests of Bell's Heat Appliances Ltd. Then, in 1935, Aga Heat itself was acquired by Allied Ironfounders Ltd. A telegram sent on 29th June 1935 by the former's Managing Director, one W. T. Wren, to notify Aga in Sweden neatly encapsulates a turning point in the history of the Aga. It read: 'OFFICIAL OFFER FROM ALLIED IRONFOUNDERS NOW RECEIVED. STOP.'

Marketing of the Aga in Britain continued apace despite such boardroom tussles. And with kitchens the length of the land converting to gas or electricity, and with the Depression starting to bite, the sales teams, firstly at Bell's Asbestos and then at Aga Heat Ltd, understood the need to win the nation's trust. Why should potential customers take the apparently backward step of investing in a solid fuel-fired range?

Earliest sales campaigns for the new product concentrated, therefore, on two issues: how the Aga – with its old-fashioned appearance – worked; and how it achieved such phenomenal fuel economy.

In a 1932 sales brochure, Bell's set out its claims for the Aga. The brochure proclaimed:

That the Aga Cooker, with a maximum fuel cost of £1 a quarter, is the most economical cooking range in the world, of any kind, gas, coal or electric.

That, since the fuel consumption of the Aga is constant and independent of the amount the Aga is used and the number it cooks for, the Aga is equally suitable and equally economical for large or small households.

That, since the Aga need be refilled only once and riddled only twice in 24 hours, it is, in fact, as convenient as any gas or electric cooker.

And that, since the exterior needs only a wet cloth and the hot plates and

Angela's got the marvellous new Aga Cooker

She actually pays

less than 25/- a quarter for fuel

And not only Angela, but nearly 10,000 women are enjoying the extra leisure, the economy, the efficiency, the cleanliness and the good cooking of the famous Aga Cooker. Independent of gas and electricity, the Aga is more economical than either. And in other ways, too, the Aga proves its claim to be the most efficient cooking stove in the world. Cleaning is easy, simple, quick. Fuelling and riddling need be done only twice a day. The Aga burns continuously night and day, which means no fire-lighting, no waiting for cooking temperature at any hour. The Aga, also, has been designed to save waiting about and continual watching of progress. Two large cooking ovens look after, *without attention*, most of the cooking usually done on top. And that means a fine clear top with a simmering plate, on which nothing can boil over, and a very hot hot-plate which brings a pint of water from cold to boiling in $1\frac{1}{2}$ minutes — far quicker than gas or electricity. There is a capacious roasting oven in which automatic heat control means no basting and less shrinkage of meat. Another very useful feature is the plate-heating oven. For washing up, vegetables and so on, there is a 10-gallon hot water tank within the cooker. The Aga Cooker has no fumes, dust or dirt—no danger of explosions, burns or shocks. Very cool and reachable, the Aga not only is delightful to cook with, but also produces delightful food. Please send for our new 36-page free Aga Book—you'll find it interesting.

Specification

Guaranteed maximum fuel cost — 25/- a quarter

Four large ovens — one roasting and baking oven, two cooking ovens, one plate-heating oven. Two hot-plates — one simmering, one boiling. Ten-gallon hot-water tank within the Cooker. Automatic heat control. Automatic safety draught control. Special fuel hopper. Easily cleaned, heat-resisting vitreous enamel surfaces. Metal parts chromium plated. All metal in

AGA (Regd Trade Mark) HEAT STORAGE COOKER

Cookery Advisory Department.

(Licensed annually by the L.C.C as a cooks' employment agency.

We have now opened a Cookery Advisory Department in the Showrooms at 20, North Audley Street. Cooks who wish to learn more about the Aga Cooker and see it in action are invited to call. It is possible for Aga Heat Ltd. to put owners and prospective owners in touch with

My memories of growing up with the very first Aga

As a little boy growing up in Beaconsfield in the late 1920s, Richard Bedwell was able to play in the kitchen at his mother's feet alongside what would become a significant part of Britain's industrial and cultural heritage – perhaps the first Aga in Great Britain.

Richard's late father, Thomas Grattan Bedwell (above) – known to the family as 'TGB' – was joint Managing Director of Bell's Asbestos & Engineering Supplies Ltd, the first importers of the Aga. In 1929, after he and Claude W. Bell, Chairman and fellow Managing Director, had secured the contract to introduce the cooker to Britain, TGB installed the very first to arrive in his own home, a modest, brick-built, post-First World War house in Ledborough Lane (pictured opposite).

ovens only a wire brush to keep the Aga bright and clean, it is as clean and labour-saving as electricity.

That the Aga is always ready for immediate use, day or night, at no extra cost... that the Aga is simple to cook on and provides all the variations in oven and hotplate temperature that modern cooking requires. That the Aga is immensely popular with servants since it is cool and comfortable to live with and very labour-saving. The fire never goes out and all the drudgery of raking out, lighting and cleaning is removed.

From the start, testimonials from new customers were deemed vital to the success of the mission to sell the new Aga. In February 1932, M. S. Frood, warden of the Helena Club in Lancaster Gate, London – later to become a venue for the Aga Cookery School – wrote extolling the virtues of a brace of new ranges. Her letter was reproduced in a sales brochure. It read:

The Aga Stoves have proved an enormous success in this Club; though we have only two, we have made a saving of over £50 in six months. When the third is installed we hope to cook entirely for our household of 150.

We make great use of the bottom ovens, using them overnight for the stock, porridge and fruit, and during the afternoons, when the cooks are off duty, for the soup, casseroles, fricasees, milk puddings and custards, all these having been cooked sufficiently on top, can be left to take care of themselves till required. A great asset we find is that the joints and birds never need be basted, and are cooked without drying up or losing weight.

And the same sales brochure quotes G. M. Boumphrey – 'an altogether praiseworthy and right-minded gentleman' – writing in

There, under the gaze of his mother, Edith, the young Richard would play cooking games. Richard says: 'My parents had the Swedes visit a number of times because they built up a good relationship. I was only two when the Aga arrived and we moved houses and went on to have lots of Agas.

'I do remember that later I used to love to play with the red ball on the front of the Aga. It was the way you told whether there was something in the Aga. That is an abiding childhood memory. I was charged with the job of turning the red ball on many occasions!'

With Claude W. Bell, Thomas Grattan Bedwell established Bell's Asbestos & Engineering Supplies Ltd in 1929 after the parent company of the same name went into bankruptcy during the Depression.

A formal minute of a meeting held four years later, on May 24 1933, records that it is 'agreed that C. W. Bell be appointed Managing Director of Bell's Heat Appliances Ltd, a company formed to handle the Aga cooker'.

Richard Bedwell himself in turn went to work for Bell's, rising to the position of Personnel Director. Now 74 and still living in Beaconsfield, he has been married for 45 years; he and his wife, Prue, have four children and 11 grand-children.

Right: perhaps the very first Aga to have been welcomed into a British home; it was installed at the Beaconsfield home (below) of Thomas Grattan Bedwell, joint MD of Bell's Asbestos & Engineering Supplies

The fictional couples used to promote the Aga in the 1930s

The early importers of the Aga to the UK used a 'family' of fictional characters to sell the concept of the new range cooker to the British public. The 1930s advertising campaign – in publications such as *Punch* – provides a fascinating insight into attitudes and social mores of the time…

MICHAEL didn't believe it. It seemed too good to be true. But Mary, who wasn't interested in the economy of the Aga so much as its labour-saving qualities and its cooking effciency, cajoled him into buying one. Now, to his surprise, he has found that it really is true that the fuel consumption of the Aga is constant – only 6cwt of coke (or anthracite) a quarter, at a cost of less than 20s. Compared with his old bill of about £7 a quarter, that saves Michael about £24 a year in the kitchen alone, Michael is pleased. Wouldn't you be?

MARY of course simply loves her Aga. What with the slump and so on, she finds herself in the kitchen a good deal these days. But the drudgery is gone. The Aga is even more labour-saving than gas and as clean as any electric stove,

The Spectator's delightfully quaint Modern Home Page. 'It is difficult to retain enthusiasm for any other type of cooker after testing the Aga,' he wrote. 'This is really indecently efficient. Its ridiculous fuel consumption means that in a fair-sized household the money actually saved in fuel bills will almost pay the hire-purchase instalments.'

Endorsement from authoritative third-parties was also important to the success of the new product. Words of praise from the trusted Good Housekeeping Institute were priceless. In 1931, Bell's Heat Appliances Ltd installed an Aga at the Institute's London offices for the purposes of 'prolonged and exhaustive tests by staff'. The subsequent typewritten report – delivered to Bell's in July 1933 – prompted the General Manager to memo all staff. 'We have seen no better exposition of the Aga's virtues,' he told his sales team, 'which, coming from so impartial a source, has great value. The report should be read and digested by all your people connected with sales, service

and erection.' The report was indeed highly praising.

This cooking stove [the Aga] has been used in the Institute for carrying out all cooking processes, including baking, boiling, steaming etc. Excellent results have been obtained and we consider the stove especially suitable for households of from 10 to 15 persons, although it would also be economical for smaller numbers. It is amazingly economical in the consumption of fuel, as well as being exceptionally clean and labour-saving. It is very simple to use, there being no dampers to regulate while cooking is in progress, and also the bases of saucepans etc remain spotlessly clean as they do not come into direct contact with the fuel.

The Aga is pleasing in appearance, and the pale cream colour in which it is enamelled would tone with any kitchen decorations.'

and is completely free from fumes or exposed heat. Besides, Mary's no expert, but the Aga makes her seem one to Michael. They've never eaten such good food before. The Aga does everything it's told and does it well and without fuss at any hour of the day or night.

PATRICK is wildly enthusiastic about their Aga. In fact, he would scarcely leave the kitchen for the first week they had it. He is fascinated by its mechanical perfection and simplicity – and can't get over the fact that the Aga really lives up to the advertised claims for it. In the first quarter, burning day and night and cooking for their household of ten, it used only 5½cwt. of anthracite.

PAMELA and Cook are bosom friends. That's because Pamela does most of the cooking since their Aga was installed, though Cook always refers to it fondly as 'My Aga'. She certainly cooks better on it than she has ever cooked before, and she's never as irritable as she used to be. That's because the Aga is so clean, so cool, so compact and so free from 'moods'. Besides, she only has to stoke it once a day, and it's alight and ready for use first thing in the morning…

By royal appointment

Once the British public had been tutored in the science of the Aga and the art of cooking on it, marketing of the product took a distinct twist, with the distributors opting for a campaign of what might be termed 'social percolation'.

The decision was taken to sell the idea of the Aga to nationally renowned institutions, dignitaries, the titled and the Royal Family and allow reputation by association to enhance the brand's standing. Brochures listed the names of those notables who had recently taken delivery of an Aga, though the distributors took care to cause no offence. 'All names,' Aga literature would state, 'are published with the express permission of the Owners. To that policy we shall always rigidly adhere.'

One such sales pamphlet from the mid-1930s includes a page entitled Some Aga Owners. It opens by listing those members of the Royal Family whose kitchens now had an Aga. They included HRH Princess Beatrice, Kensington Palace; HRH Princess Alice, Countess of Athlone, Kensington Palace and Brantridge Park, Sussex; HH Princess Helena Victoria; and HH Princess Marie Louise. Other notables included in the list of 55 new owners were the Earl of Buckinghamshire, Mary, the Duchess of Hamilton, Admiral of the Fleet Sir Roger Keyes, General Sir Archibald A. Montgomery-Massingbird and the Earl Nelson.

The listing of notable institutions to have taken delivery of an Aga – or, in many cases, several of them – indicates how quickly the new range became established in large kitchens. By the mid-1930s, Eton College and Harrow School both had Model J 1734 heavy-duty cookers. The canteens at the Woolwich Arsenal in East London, Trinity Hall, Dublin, King's College Hospital in London, and the Royal Western Yacht Club in Plymouth were all catering on Aga cookers.

St Mary's Hostel for Women in Papworth had an Aga installed, as did the Convent of Our Lady's Bower in County Kildare, St Bride's Nursing Home in Galway, the Green Parrot Restaurant and

The sisters of Holy Cross Convent in Gerrards Cross were among the earliest users of the Aga in Britain. Though the convent is now a school, some of the older members of the order still fondly remember the cooker's arrival

The Aga Cookery School and the venerable Ambrose Heath

Aga Heat Ltd – manufacturer and distributor of the Aga through the second half of the 1930s – established a Cookery Advisory Department at its showrooms in North Audley Street in London's West End. The Principal of the academy, where new Aga cooks could attend lectures and discuss issues with trained staff, was Mabel Collins, M.C.A., First Class Diplomee, N.T.S.C. A brochure of the time sold the benefits of enrolling…

'We know the culinary possibilities of the Aga are infinite and we hope to do our best by this means to bring them home to every one of our Aga users.

'In addition to our trained staff, we have been lucky in securing the services of Mr. Ambrose Heath, the famous writer on cookery subjects to the *Morning Post* and other papers, as Gastronomical Adviser to Aga Heat Ltd. Here is an opportunity to enlist the willing aid of an expert in solving all your cooking problems.'

Ambrose Heath went on to write the first Aga cookbook. *Good Food on the Aga* – published by Faber & Faber with illustrations by Edward Bawden and costing 7s.6d. net or 8s. from Aga outlets – has become highly collectable, a mint copy in 2002 commanding a three-figure price.

the Jewish Maternity Hospital in London, the Holy Cross Convent in Gerrards Cross and the Royal National Institute for the Blind at St Leonards and Chorleywood.

At Cardiff Royal Infirmary, no fewer than twelve Agas were installed, lending the kitchen the appearance of a vast food factory.

'It has revolutionised cooking'

Converts to the Aga cause quickly became vocal evangelists, many writing to distributors to praise their new acquisitions.

'I cannot praise the Aga cooker too highly: it is the only thing I have ever bought that is better than the advertisement says it is,' wrote Mr Harvey Hilliard, CBE, MD, of Clarendon Place, London.

'I am very pleased with the Aga cooker,' wrote another correspondent, Mrs E. M. Evans, of Holland Villas Road in Kensington, London. 'I have not only recommended it to my friends… [but] can assure you that we cannot praise it enough, and it may interest you to know that even my housemaid, when talking of

it yesterday, said it had quite revolutionised cooking.'

By 1935, marketing of the Aga had become big business and the autumn launch of the New Standard Aga – a 3-feet 3-inches-wide twin-oven model in cream aimed at owners of smaller kitchens – saw Aga Heat Ltd embark on a nationwide publicity campaign to raise awareness of the brand within a much broader audience.

In the same year, Aga Heat Ltd commissioned its colourful sales representative in Scotland to write a guide to selling the Aga.

David Ogilvy's *The Theory and Practice of Selling the Aga Cooker* became the company's sales 'bible' and has become a piece of history in its own right; *Fortune* magazine has described it as 'the best sales manual ever written'. Its author – after emigrating to the United States – went on to become the most influential advertising executive of the post-war period, in 1948 founding the agency now known worldwide as Ogilvy & Mather.

In his sales manual, Ogilvy –

The "New Standard" AGA COOKER

(Regd Trade Mark)

gives you
better cooking, more leisure . .
a Guaranteed maximum fuel cost
of less than £4 a year

Some points of the "New Standard" AGA Cooker:

The most economical in the world.

Independent of gas or electricity.

Burns day and night.

No morning fires to light.

Easy to clean, simple to manage.

Always ready for immediate use.

No fumes, or cooking smells.

Extremely rapid boiling, safe simmering.

All cooking temperatures automatically controlled.

Two big ovens, two large hot-plates.

The Aga and the father of modern advertising

David Ogilvy (1911-1999) was a pivotal figure in the success of the Aga in the mid-1930s. He was born David Mackenzie Ogilvy in West Horsley, England, on June 23, 1911, and was educated at Fettes College in Edinburgh and at Christ Church, Oxford, though he did not graduate.

The son of a Surrey stockbroker, he was Aga's first Scottish sales representative and went on to join Mather and Crowther, the advertising agency which was to secure the Aga account and create many of Aga's seminal marketing campaigns of the time. In 1938, he emigrated to the United States.

After the Second World War – during which he worked for British Intelligence out of the Washington Embassy – he founded the agency now known as Ogilvy & Mather. Starting in 1948 with no clients and a staff of two, he built the company into a worldwide enterprise – one of the eight largest agency networks.

David Ogilvy retired to Touffou, a fourteenth-century chateau in France, in 1973 and died in 1999.

Facing page: one of Ogilvy's seminal Aga advertisements

often described as somewhat brash in his manner – offered earnest, pragmatic advice to his peers on how best to command the attention of the customer and, subsequently, secure a sale. His foreword began:

In Great Britain there are twelve million households. One million of these own motorcars. Only ten thousand own Aga Cookers. No household which can afford a motorcar can afford to be without an Aga. There are certain universal rules. Dress quietly and shave well. Do not wear a bowler hat. Go to the back door (most salesmen go to the front door, a manoeuvre always resented by maid and mistress alike).

Tell the person who opens the door frankly and briefly what you have come for; it will get her on your side. Never on any account get in on false pretences.

Study the best time of day for calling; between 12.00 and 2pm you will not be welcome, whereas a call at an unorthodox time – after supper in the summer for instance – will often succeed. In general, study the methods of your competitors and do the exact opposite.

Find out all you can about your prospects before you call on them; their general living conditions, wealth, profession, hobbies, friends and so on. Every hour spent on this kind of research will help you and impress your prospect.

The worst fault a salesman can commit is to be a bore... Pretend to be vastly interested in any subject the prospect shows an interest in. The more she talks the better, and if you can make her laugh you are several points up. Perhaps the most important thing of all is to avoid standardisation in your sales talk. If you find yourself one day saying the same things to a

Ode to the Aga...

Amusing – though not always particularly proficient – poems were often a feature of 1930s advertising campaigns for the Aga. The following is typical of a type designed – in the words of an Aga executive – to appeal to the mass market "mail-order type"…

Let's Talk of Food

"Let's talk of food," said Agatha,
        "we wives
Can learn a lot from one another's
        lives.
We're sober married women – don't
        we look it?
Let's talk of what we eat and how
        we cook it."
"Thomas," said Kate, "is fond of
        chops and lager,
Rump steak and chips; we cook
        them on the Aga."
"Now Joe's a soldier bold," said
        Joan, "a Major.
He likes the best – and gets it, from
        an Aga."
"Jack is a dramatist," said Jill, "and
        vaguer..!
Meals when ready…so we use an
        Aga."
Said Susan: "Simon's just a carpet
        bagger,
Poor but particular; we've got an
        Aga."
"Our income's small; our children
        daily larger,"
Said Mary, "but we manage with an
        Aga."

DÉJEUNER SUR L'HERBE by EDOUARD MANET (1832-1883). Manet was born in Paris and entered Couture's studio at the age of 19. Though his independence infuriated his master and his pictures were constantly rejected by the Salon, he soon gathered a group of painters round him, Whistler and Fantin-Latour among them. In 1863, when Napoleon III ordered the establishment of a Salon des Refusés, Manet's " Déjeuner sur l'herbe," which afterwards exercised a tremendous influence on Cézanne, was its scandal and success. It is reproduced, by permission, from the painting in the Louvre.

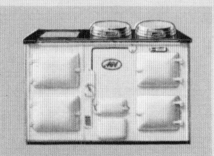

THIS picture caused a public scandal in 1863. Manet's subject was shocking, people complained: though actually, of course, it was their conservatism that was outraged — not their moral sensibilities. The real offence of the picture was that it stood for something new : and at that time whatever was new was certain to be opposed. Later in the century scientific innovations, such as the first telephones and motor cars, were attacked with the same conservative fury. Nowadays, fortunately, we are better tuned to progress. Eight years ago, for instance, when the revolutionary Aga Cooker was introduced, people were quick to appreciate its advantages : its cream and chromium cleanliness ; guaranteed maximum fuel consumption ; readiness for work by day and night and gift of meeting cooks three-quarters of the way. Already this cooker has brought a new reign of comfort and good temper to more than 20,000 kitchens.

AGA HEAT LIMITED, 20 NORTH AUDLEY STREET, W.1.
(Proprietors: Allied Ironfounders Ltd.)

AGA COOKER

AFRICA—Aga Heat (Africa) (Pty.) Ltd., P.O. Box 7058, JOHANNESBURG, also at DURBAN and CAPE TOWN. BRITISH WEST INDIES—Bermuda Engineering Co. Ltd., HAMILTON, BERMUDA. CANADA—Aga (Canada) Ltd., 431, King Street West, TORONTO. CEYLON—Walker & Greig, Ltd., COLOMBO. INDIA—Wm. Jacks & Co., BOMBAY, CALCUTTA, KARACHI, MADRAS, DELHI, LAHORE, and RANGOON. NEW ZEALAND—Levin & Co., Ltd., Corner of Featherston and Ballance streets, WELLINGTON. *The word AGA is the Registered Trade Mark of Aga Heat Ltd.*

A recipe from the archives

Ambrose Heath – resident Aga chef and nutritionist in the 1930s and author of the highly collectable *Good Food on the Aga* – was also editor of the *Aga Quarterly*, forerunner of the still-popular *Aga Magazine*.

In it, the respected epicurean wrote of food, recipes and his love affair with the English seasons. In the Summer 1937 edition, he turned his pen toward Nature's most bountiful times and offered an interesting suggestion on how to use up the shank end of a ham…

The End of the Ham

Few things are more disconcerting than the shank end of a ham which refuses to get finished up. This

bishop and a trapezist, you are done for. When the prospect tries to bring the interview to a close, go gracefully. It can only hurt you to be kicked out.

Ogilvy divided his advice into two sections: attack and defence. He began the former with what he called a general statement.

'Most people,' he wrote, 'have heard something about the Aga Cooker. They vaguely believe it to involve some new method of cooking. They may have heard that it works on the principle of heat storage. Heat storage is the oldest known form of cooking. Aborigines bake their hedgehogs in the ashes of a dying fire.'

Ogilvy went on to offer guidance on the wisdom or otherwise of what he called 'wise-cracking'.

The longer you talk to a prospect the better, and you will not do this if you are a bore. Pepper your talk with anecdotes and jokes. Accumulate a repertoire of illustration. A deadly serious

demonstration is bound to fail. If you can't make a lady laugh, you certainly cannot make her buy. Above all, laugh till you cry every time the prospect makes the joke about the Aga Khan!

Interviewed for a BBC documentary in 1997, just a few years before his death, Ogilvy reminisced on his time as an Aga salesman.

It [the Aga] became part of upper-crust life in England. You have a shooting stick, you have a spaniel, you send your children to some ghastly boarding school and you have an Aga.

We started selling from the top down; sort of a snob status symbol. I will never forget old Queen Mary coming to have a look at it and someone telling her that one of the royal aunts – I forget which, one of the old princesses – had been given one free because she had

Thirties advertising sold the idea that the Aga would make the housewife's life easier and more pleasurable

been so kind to us. And Queen Mary was furious that this royal aunt had gotten one free because her second son – the Duke of York, later George VI, Bertie – had to pay for his.

We got them into stately homes. One stately home sold another stately home. I had to go round to these stately homes and I always went to the back door. I started with the cook – I found that worked better. If I went to the front door and the Marchioness wanted to buy an Aga, the cook would shoot me down in flames because she resented the fact that I had gone behind her back.'

Ogilvy remained fond of the cooker he had done so much to promote. 'It was purely functional…entirely practical. He [Gustaf Dalén] made it as efficient as he could and…because no lousy, fancy-pants industrial designer ever worked his will on it, it remains an honest-to-God

functional thing. It was a special kind of modernity. It wasn't a fad, a passing fancy. It looked solid, was solid and is solid. It was the Rolls-Royce of the kitchen and people realised that very quickly.'

The competition heats up

The Aga did not, however, have 1930s Britain to itself. Several iron founders were quick to pounce on the opportunity to market competitors to the new style of cooker and most took space in magazines of the day to stress the 'all-British' nature of their rival products.

R. Taylor & Company, of Larbert in Stirlingshire, took a quarter-page advertisement in the September 1939 edition of *Good Housekeeping* magazine to promote its Tayco-Ette cooker and boiler unit, which boasted 'two ovens, constant hot water, a large surface hob, a hot closet and low fuel costs'. In all-black finish, the unit sold for £17.50s.; enamelled with a nickel-plated hotplate and base, it was priced at £23.10s.

The London Warming Company, of Rathbone Place in London's

ingenious, and very pleasant, dish solves this tiresome problem. Make some paste with a pound of flour, two ounces of butter, a beaten egg and a gill of thick sour cream.

Cut this into several pieces, roll them out thin, and use some of it to line the bottom and sides of a cake tin which has first been buttered. Mince up your ham, lean and fat together (but do not overdo the fat) and mince an onion with it. You should have a soup-plate full.

Now beat up five eggs with half a pint of cream. Mix them with the ham and onion and season with salt, pepper and nutmeg. Spread a finger-thick layer of this paste on the pastry at the bottom of the tin, cover this with a very thin layer of pastry, then more ham, more pastry, and so on until you close the tin with a top layer of pastry.

An hour in a hot oven will cook it and it should be served turned out, with a sauce if you wish.

AMBROSE HEATH

Facing page: the British kitchen goes thoroughly modern in an Aga brochure from September 1933

West End, offered the Kooksjoie anthracite range for 'continuous hot water and perfect cooking'. The Foresight Ther-co-Oven, by Samuel Smith & Sons of Smethwick, looked more like the Aga of its day, though its square hotplate covers opened to the left and right, rather than up and back, and it was designed, at £27 complete, to appeal to even 'the most modest purse'. The Triplex Foundry, in Great Bridge in Staffordshire, (with showrooms in London, Birmingham and Manchester) launched its Triplex 24 – 'one fire for all the cooking and hot water'. And the AB Cooker – promoted by Federated Foundries Ltd of Mayfair – promised a fuel consumption of no more than three tons a year.

But in the early days of Aga's mission to conquer the kitchens of Britain, it was the Esse Cooker Company, owned by Smith & Wellstood Ltd and based in Bonnybridge in Scotland, which was to provide the keenest competition. Its Premier Esse was offered on hire purchase from 17s. a month over four years, with a

'model to suit every household'. The Esse, like the Aga, ran on smokeless fuel – anthracite or coke – and burned continuously, promising, as the company's advertisements proclaimed, 'independence from public power supply services'.

It differed from the Aga in having only one hotplate, but did offer a front-mounted thermostat to ensure 'not only the exact cooking temperature at any time, but remarkable fuel economy'.

In response, Aga Heat Ltd continued to advertise heavily its twin-oven, double-hotplate Model C and its marketing campaign increasingly focused on appealing directly to housewives. In the October 1939 edition of *Good Housekeeping* magazine – just a month after Prime Minister Neville Chamberlain had announced the declaration of war on Germany – a full-page advertisement cited four women whose 'lives had been made all the happier through the purchase of an Aga'.

By November 1940, with formal food rationing still two months away, advertisements for the Aga

And it's good for seal meat!

From 1934 to 1937, an Aga performed sterling service with members of a British team surveying the Antarctic. In an advertisement in *Punch* from December 1937, John Rymill, leader of the British Graham Land Expedition, described how the cooker helped reduce the tedium of their rather limited meals. 'We took an Aga Cooker to the Antarctic in 1934. There were 16 of us. For three years the Aga did all our cooking. It turned out to be foolproof. It coaxed new flavour from our perennial seal meat.'

Installations large and small

'I started working with Agas in 1938. I was 16 and was taken on as an ironmonger/fitter by Robert Pochin Ltd, of Granby Street in Leicester, who were distributors for Aga Heat Ltd as it was then. We worked a 40-mile radius around Leicester. I must have installed hundreds of Agas. I remember we installed one Aga into this house which had a kitchen that must have been no more than six feet square. I swear that if the owner faced the Aga and then turned round she would have been in the sink.

'I also remember we installed an Aga at the home of Lady Barnet, of television's *What's My Line?* She was a lovely lady.'

trevor limon, 78, OF CURRY RIVEL, LANGPORT, IN SOMERSET

nevertheless began to reflect the changing mood of the nation and the growing need for everyone to 'do their bit'. 'The Government asks for fuel economy,' read one advertisement, 'the Aga provides it. Complete freedom from breakdowns or emergencies.'

And Aga Heat Ltd started to hit back at its rivals: 'The Aga is the original heat storage cooker. It is British made throughout.' Later the same month, the advertising had been refined further. The British Government's emergency Fuel and Lighting Order had required household consumption of electricity, coal and gas to be reduced by 25 per cent and Aga Heat Ltd responded quickly: 'The Aga cooker ensures a year's cooking on less than the minimum Government fuel ration. It is invaluable in households where National Service causes irregular meals because it "keeps in" continuously night and day.'

And so, as the decade drew to a close and the shadow of war slowly crept across the Channel, the Aga steeled itself for its next challenge: battling for Britain on the home front…

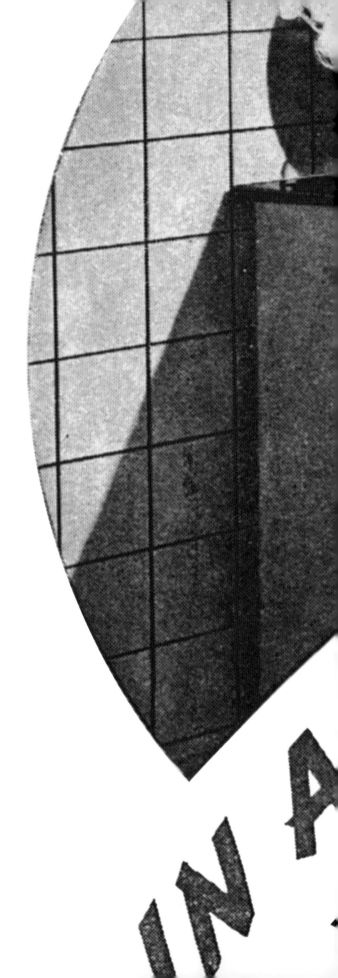

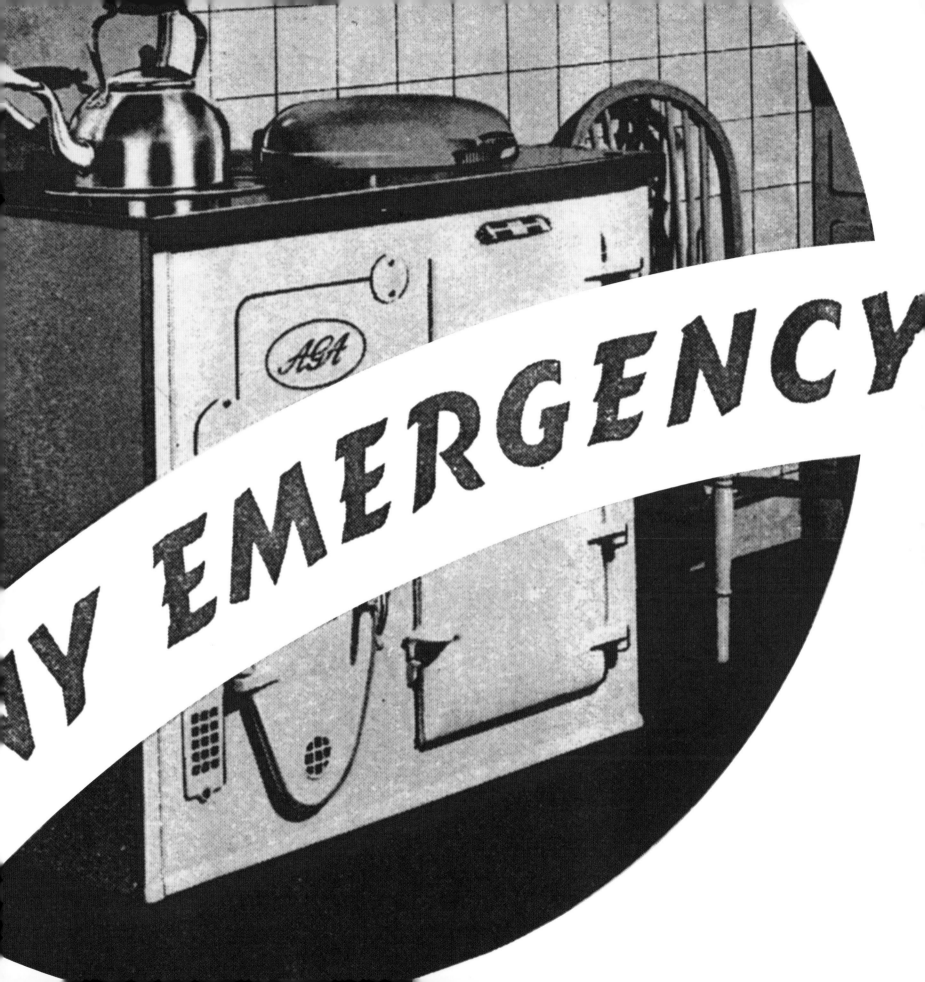

1940-1949

The Aga goes to war

Despite the war tearing the planet apart in the early days of the Aga's third decade, Aga Heat Ltd continued to strive to meet demand for its cookers from the nation's housewives, who themselves were fighting their own battles on the vital home front. Indeed, the Aga – with its efficient use of fuel and its continuous heat source free from the vagaries of the supply of gas or electricity – was seen as something of a boon.

In a magazine advertising campaign entitled '4 Wives Solve Wartime Problems with the Aga', those virtues were sold through the voices of a quartet of fictional stiff-upper-lipped characters:

'Mrs A has to watch her expenses very carefully. But she knows exactly where she stands with her cooking costs – for her Aga Cooker cannot burn more than its fixed amount of fuel, and it is the most economical cooker in the world,' opened the campaign.

Others, meanwhile, had to struggle with varying meal times.

'Mrs B's husband is a warden, liable to get home at all hours, and wanting a good hot meal. Mrs B often has cause to bless the fact that the Aga Cooker is always 'in', day and night, and has a wonderful simmering oven that keeps food hot and unspoiled for hours on end.

'Mrs C's husband is overseas and she has the two children with her. Her Aga cooks their food for them just as well as it can be cooked, and it will not let her down in an emergency. The Aga Cooker is entirely independent and self-contained.'

Finally, there was Mrs D, coping admirably with a houseful…

'Four evacuees are staying with Mrs D. A lot of extra work and a lot of extra meals. But the Aga practically works itself, and a rub with a damp cloth keeps it clean. The Aga Cooker needs only five minutes' attention a day.'

But while the war raged, peace apparently broke out between Aga Heat Ltd, still based in London's West End, and its arch rival, the Esse Cooker Company, of Bonnybridge in Scotland. By October of 1940, the two companies had formed something of a strategic alliance and were advertising their respective cookers together in the same press advertisements. 'Lucky are the people with an Aga

or an Esse,' a typical advertisement began. 'Irregular wartime meals cannot make their fuel bills rise.'

Gone was the sniping sales patter of previous, competitive, campaigns. The two companies were now allies: 'The fuel consumptions of these famous heat storage cookers remain unchanged from quarter to quarter…Some of these cookers are still available, despite present manufacturing limitations.'

In 1941 – with the Nazis in Russia and with London still in the grip of the Blitz – Aga Heat Ltd withdrew from production all Aga models and replaced them with a range of cookers with standardised parts. This applied to domestic models and the heavy-duty units installed in such well-known institutions as Eton College, Harrow School, Westminster Abbey Choir School and Cardiff Royal Infirmary.

These heavy-duty Agas were gargantuan slabs of interlocking iron. Designed to cater for up to 130, they dominated the busy kitchens in schools, convents, nursing homes, hospitals and military messes. At Eton College, the Model J 1734 ran the length of one wall of the kitchen. It boasted an extra-rapid boiling plate, two further boiling plates, a simmering plate (all with square lids), a roasting oven, baking oven and simmering oven. It promised a guaranteed maximum fuel consumption of 10 tons a year, burning coke, anthracite or Phurnacite.

When the war came, much of Aga Heat Ltd's production of Agas had been diverted to help the war effort. Government contracts were limiting severely the number of cookers available for domestic use, and by 1942 the waiting list for a new Aga was such that the company – now owned by Allied Ironfounders Ltd of Coalbrookdale in Shropshire, where the Aga is still made today – decided to explain why in print.

In the February edition of *Good Housekeeping* magazine – under the headline 'Why must I wait for my Aga? Because war services cannot wait.' – it ran a public service announcement which, in its own right, was a clever piece of

MINISTRY

OF FOOD

THE WEEK'S

FOOD

FACTS No. 7

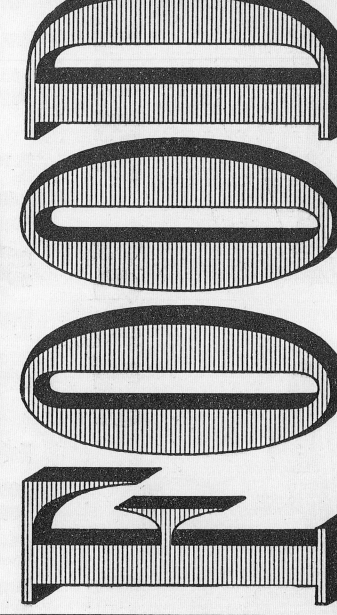

Tear out this advertisement and pin it up in your kitchen with the others in the series.

What do I do...

if I have no shelter for myself and family?

I know that in my house there is one room which provides reasonable protection against the dangers of air attack, but that protection can be improved. So the first thing

...and for building or rebuilding our bodies. But do you know that we can eat also to *protect ourselves from illness?* Science has discovered that some foods rich in vitamins and mineral salts increase resistance to infections.

All the foods in the panel below are of this kind: they are nature's "tonics" and nature's "medicines". They should be part of your diet as much as the *protective foods.* They are nature's body-building and energy foods. Begin to eat wisely now for the sake of your health in the winter.

ON THE KITCHEN FRONT

Do you listen-in to the hints and recipes given at 8.15 every morning on the Wireless?

A NEW SALAD. Wash and drain a crisp lettuce, put it in a bowl and pour over it a dressing made by mixing thoroughly 2 tablespoonfuls salad oil, 1 tablespoonful vinegar with salt and pepper to taste. Turn the lettuce over and over in the dressing with a wooden spoon; then line your bowl with it. Pile in the middle a grated raw carrot, a chopped apple, a cupful of cooked diced potatoes, and decorate with chopped mint and a small chopped onion.

THE BLACKBERRY CROP.

Blackberries are ripening fast all over the country. Don't neglect this good and health-

---

HOW TO DRY PLUMS.

The whole secret of drying plums is in drying them *slowly.* First wash your fruit and arrange on muslin-covered racks or wire trays. Dry as slowly as possible, at never more than 120°F. Use, on several consecutive days, the heat left in your oven after cooking. Keep the oven

---

buy a book (price 3d.) called "YOUR HOME AS AN AIR RAID SHELTER," which tells me how to choose the best place in the house and how to improve it. I can get this book at any Post Office, order it from any newsagent or (by sending 4d. in stamps) obtain it direct from H.M. Stationery Office, Kingsway, London, W.C.2. *I do it now* because the safety of my family and myself may depend on my action.

Cut this out—and keep it!

Issued by The Ministry of Information Space presented to the Nation by The Brewers' Society

---

Britain in the grip of rationing...

Even before the outbreak of the Second World War, the British Government had devised a scheme – known as the Food Defence Plans – to be introduced if it became necessary. Within a week of war being declared, a separate government department was inaugurated, the Ministry of Food. It was to employ some 50,000 officials and at its head was the the Minister of Food, Lord Woolton. A gifted orator and a skilled broadcaster, he was to become a trusted and respected figure amongst Britain's housewives.

Ration books for adults and children had already been printed as a precautionary measure, but food rationing and the issuing of ration books was not introduced until after the war broke out. Unusual as it may seem now, the government conducted an opinion poll to see if such a course of action would be accepted by the general public.

January 1940 saw the introduction of the first food rationing to war-torn Britain. Bacon, butter and sugar were affected first, swiftly followed by limits on meat, fish, tea, jam, biscuits, breakfast cereals, cheese, eggs, milk and canned fruit.

Paradoxically, of course, rationing had an important side-effect: the system enforced a balanced diet and, as a consequence, the health of the nation improved during the

marketing.

'If there is some delay in the delivery of your Aga Cooker,' it began, 'it is because so many are now required for canteens in munition works, in hospitals and communal feeding centres.'

And the advertisement called on the Aga community to continue to show forebearance, certain in the knowledge they were, indirectly, doing their bit for King and country: 'You will be patient, knowing the life-long benefits that your Aga will bring when it *does* come.'

Having been encouraged before the outbreak of war to make the move to gas and electricity, British housewives suddenly found themselves being bombarded with advice from the new Ministry of Food and Power. Use only one bar at a time on the electric fire, they were ordered, cook on the smallest gas ring and use only five inches of water when any member of the family takes a bath.

In 1943, with Britain's menfolk fighting, working in essential factories or tilling the soil, all women aged between 18 and 45 were required to work part-time,

providing for many an independence never before experienced.

There was no drop-off in demand for Agas during the war years. In Britain, it was still the case that few houses were centrally-heated and – with a dearth of servants to call upon – more and more landed wives were, perhaps for the first time, having to do much of the cooking themselves. In their large and draughty country houses, many found the Aga a life-saver during the hard times.

Still waiting on jam tomorrow

The 'jam tomorrow' optimism which sustained many during the war – founded on the belief that better times were just around the corner – evaporated in the financial crisis that gripped the nation as a direct result of massive wartime spending. Rationing continued and, despite the post-war baby-boom, the divorce rate increased ten-fold.

Progress was slow, but 86 per cent of homes had electricity by 1948, the New Town Act paved the way for the construction of up to four million new homes for bombed Britain, and farmers found

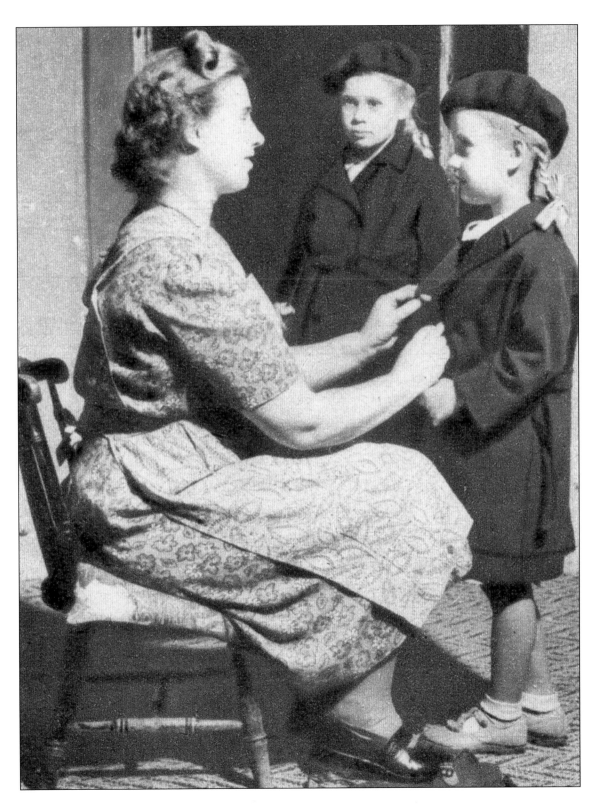

period. Children were treated differently and were entitled to extra foods, such as milk and orange juice, considered essential for growth. The National Milk Scheme provided one pint of milk for every child under five. Expectant mothers and young children were entitled to free milk if the combined income of parents was less than 40 shillings a week.

Britons keen to support the war effort were encouraged to grow their own food. The government's now-famous Dig for Victory campaign called for every family to keep an allotment. Lawns and flower-beds were turned over for vegetable gardens and chickens, rabbits, goats and pigs were reared in urban gardens across Britain.

Most foods were rationed by their weight or by a points system. Sugar was rationed at 12 ounces per week, but meat was rationed by cost, with each Briton allocated 1s.10d. worth of meat per week. They were also permitted 3 pints of milk, 8 ounces of sugar, 4 ounces of butter or fat, 4 ounces of bacon, 2 ounces of tea, 1 ounce of cheese and one egg. Each member of the family had their own ration book: adults had a buff-coloured book, while children over three had a blue copy and babies a green book.

If there was an excess of any product at the warehouses then the points for that product would be lowered meaning that the individual could buy more for each coupon. Conversely, if an item was in short supply, the value of its points would be raised so that each coupon would buy less.

Tea was not restricted until July 1940. Fish, although never rationed, was almost non existent during the war, and for the first time the British were introduced to tuna, snook and whale meat. There was always a constant supply of vegetables and bread production was maintained.

When wheat and flour were in short supply, millers ground more of the husks into the flour to make it go further. It may have looked less appetizing, but it was far more nutritious. In fact, white bread was prohibited because the Ministry of Food stated that it did not contain enough vitamins – a move which led directly to the introduction of the famous Hovis brown loaf.

A guide to the cost of living in 1940

In the 1940s, a two-oven Model CB Aga would have set you back the princely sum of £103, although hire purchase was available on weekly instalments. In order to understand that price tag, however, it is helpful to place it in context.

The self-raising flour necessary for baking in the Aga would have cost the 1940s housewife around 7d. per 3lb bag, while, if he was a smoker, her husband would have had to

themselves at the forefront of political initiatives to improve British agriculture.

These were, however, heady times for the Aga: by the end of the decade more than 50,000 British households boasted an Aga and demand remained buoyant. Indeed such was demand for the Aga in the years immediately after the war that Aga Heat Ltd was compelled to explain what it was doing about the backlog of orders that had built up.

The company publicised the fact that it was 'diverting to export trade most of the current production of Heavy-Duty Aga Cookers. [Secondly,] a greatly increased proportion of domestic Aga cooker output is being sent abroad.

'Both these valuable exports,' the policy document explained, 'will help to buy you food, your tobacco and raw materials for your industry. The steamer lane to foreign markets is the way, the immediate way, to national and indeed personal survival.'

The Aga Heat policy document added that priority would be given

to farmers and doctors and that the measures were necessary because of the 'backlog of orders for Aga cookers and water heaters being so great that the earliest delivery date for any normal order received must, at present rate of production, be set at save 27 months ahead'.

In 1947, Allied Ironfounders Ltd – owners of Aga Heat Ltd – took decisive action to close the gap between public demand for the Aga and its ability to produce them. It decided to increase production by adding to its plant in Smethwick a second plant at Ketley near Telford in Shropshire.

Production was to continue at Smethwick until 1957, when all manufacture would switch to Ketley. Together, the two plants helped define the success of the modern Aga. At the height of production, the ironfounders at Smethwick, employing up to 100, produced 200 Agas per week; while at Ketley, 175 per week were cast. Between them, they also produced up to 20 Heavy-Duty Aga ranges.

In 1946, Arthur Price (pictured above) was taken on by Albert Sykes, Works Director at the Smethwick foundry, as a layout designer and industrial engineer.

His job, at the tender age of 27, was to design the new foundry layout at Ketley, on the site of the former James Clay agricultural machinery factory where now stand the Aga-Rayburn offices, its research and development facility, training centre, despatch warehouse and enamelling shop.

Five decades on, Arthur Price – who, during his 42 years with Aga, rose through the ranks to become Managing Director at the Ketley plant and an important man in the surrounding industrial community – remembers those days well.

There wasn't a concrete floor in the place. What machinery there was – and there was very little – was just stuck on a block of concrete, so every floor had to be concreted which, in itself was quite a job.

In the winter of 1947, on 4th January, it started to snow and I was coming over here on the Monday by train to measure up and supervise what was going on. It started snowing on the 4th and it didn't stop for three months. I cleared the outside foundations so many times – the snow would stop briefly, melt and then it would start again. It was one of the worst winters I can remember.

They were such exciting times. Aga had to expand as quickly as it could. During the war a hell of a backlog built up and that was the reason for Ketley. Aga at Smethwick was in the industrial part of Smethwick and was totally enclosed. There

pay 7d. for a packet of 10 Players cigarettes. If they were to decide on an evening out, a cinema ticket would have cost 5d., while a trip to the theatre would have meant forking out 1s.6d.

If they were fortunate enough to have been able to afford staff, a live-in maid could be employed for £1 while if the housework fell to them alone, a brand new Hotpoint 500 electric vacuum cleaner would have cost £10.17s.

A Bexley dining room suit in French walnut, from Oetzman of Tottenham Court Road, was priced at 22 guineas or £4 with 12 monthly payments of £1.12d.7s. A Morris 10 motor car would have cost £195.

Back in the kitchen, a pound of butter would have cost around 1s.6d., margarine was 6d. per lb and Cheddar cheese 10d. per lb. Danish side bacon cost 1s.6d. per lb, while a pint of milk would have been 3d.

Finally, a bottle of Larola face and hand cream ('Larola makes and keeps the skin delightfully smooth, prevents roughness, redness and chaps and thus adds immeasurably to your beauty, charm and comfort. ARP wardens, women on munitions and other war workers will find Larola a wonderful protection for the complexion and for keeping hands soft, white and smooth…') had a price tag of 1s/6d a bottle.

was nowhere to put an extension on anywhere.

Arthur Price recalls with fondness his meetings with W. T. Wren, the founding Managing Director of Aga Heat. Known affectionately as 'Freckles' Wren, he had a profound impact on the young engineer.

> He was a fantastic character. He was a big man in his attitude and his thoughts and a very nice man. When he met me first he put me at ease and I was only a lad. I had a lot of respect for him.
>
> He had taken a cooker nobody knew and taken it to the stage where Smethwick was producing a lot of cookers. He had that much faith in it. He and the board at that particular time – W. T. Wren, Bowyer, the financial man, and Robbie Eliot, sales – were the architects of the modern Aga

The job of establishing a second foundry at Ketley took six months, from September 1946 to March 1947. Arthur Price:

> I suppose I was a little daunted at the time, but it was so exciting and such a big move for me to get the job and to be working for a man like Albert Sykes; he was my mentor. He could be a tough man with the wrong people, but we just hit it off.
>
> The other thing was that Albert Sykes had

joined the company shortly after my father at Smethwick and my father, Arthur Senior, had done so much for him in bringing him on in the foundry area because he was a production man, that he had time for me.

> My father was foundry manager at Smethwick. I trained as a structural and mechancial engineer, but I didn't want to be stuck in an office all my life and I wanted to get into management. I was quite ambitious at that time. And my father came in one night at said 'I've got just the job for you'. I said: 'Well, I wouldn't mind having a go at that!' He arranged an interview and a couple of days later he let my father know; we fixed my starting salary of £400 a year and I was absolutely delighted. It was double what I was getting!
>
> There was nothing unusual then about following one's father into the foundry. My father was one of twelve brothers and two sisters and all of them worked at the same foundry. They all worked for Triplex Grates.

Mr Price Senior worked at Smethwick until it closed in 1957. Up to that point, the Smethwick plant had been producing the heavier iron work, the Aga top-plates and front-plates, while Ketley produced the doors, the interior ironwork and the ovens themselves. Initially, the cookers were assembled at either plant; later, all assembly work was carried out at the Allied Ironfounders plant at

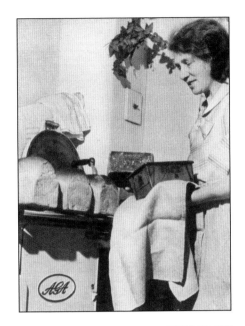

Shades of Aga life: Mrs Cole – "a committee member of Cumberland WI" – and the Shepherds of Home Farm, Bridge-of-Don, near Aberdeen

Coalbrookdale (which in the early 1970s was to take over full production of the Aga).

> During the war we were limited in how many Agas we could produce. I can't remember how many, but it was something like 20 to 30 a week and that's how the backlog built up. When the war finished the delivery period at the rate we were making them was something like five years.

Arthur Price Junior also remembers how during the war – when production of the Aga was restricted and the Smethwick foundry was partly turned over to the manufacture of grenades and shells – a slab of scrap cast iron from the Aga foundries helped save his life.

> I remember helping my father build an air-raid shelter. My father wasn't allowed a conventional shelter because he was better paid, so we dug out a great big hole in the bottom of the garden at home in Tipton and we lined the sides with nine inches of concrete and had an emergency exit which was really only a hole on the side to crawl out of with a cast-iron door – I think it was a piece of Aga scrap iron – and we lived there many, many nights because we were really trounced during the war.
>
> One bomb dropped – a high-explosive thing that came down by parachute – and that exploded about 200 yards away. And another one dropped on the doctor's surgery and killed the doctor. But the shelter served us well.

Joining the land battle

As outlined in Aga Heat Ltd's Four-Point Crisis Policy, farmers looking to instal an Aga were given priority in the years after the war. Indeed farming folk quickly became the bedrock of the Aga customer base, because the continuing absence of piped gas

Driven to distraction

W.T. Wren, the colourful Managing Director of Aga Heat Ltd, was driven everywhere by his chauffeur in a Rolls Royce bearing the personalised licence plate AGA 1. Those not in the know believed, on seeing the distinctive car, that the famous passenger inside was the Aga Khan.

Indeed when the Rolls was spotted on one occasion at a race meeting, the London *Evening Standard* promptly published a piece about the prince's exploits on the turf.

When 'Freckles' Wren's chauffeur, John, made a formal complaint regarding the case of mistaken identity – fearing he would one day wrongly be accused of unauthorised use of the car – the *Standard* printed a retraction pointing out that the Aga Khan had not, in fact, made the trip to the races. 'Rather,' it read, 'it was the makers of a very famous cooker. Need we say more!'

Right: the Aga's 1949 Farming Families pamphlet

Overleaf: Among those profiled in the pamphlet were Philip and Ruby Garrod of Little Blakenham in Suffolk

in more remote areas made solid-fuel ranges a necessity.

In 1949, four years after the end of the war, farming and the need for greater agricultural efficiency had beome a priority, so that Britain might never again be at the mercy of blockades.

Aga Heat Ltd – in conjunction with its advertising agency, Mather & Crowther – embarked on an ambitious project that was to provide a compelling marketing brochure which still, more than six decades later, provides a fascinating insight into rural British life.

For eight weeks, a team of writers and photographers made an 8,000-mile tour around the British Isles to 'record a change…which we believe is as much of a landmark in the development of British agriculture as the coming of the tractor, the combine harvester or the farmhouse telephone'.

The change, specifically, was the arrival of the Aga as an indispensable tool of the working farm and, more generally, 'the new difficulties that have arisen for the farmer's wife and her own particular forms, if not

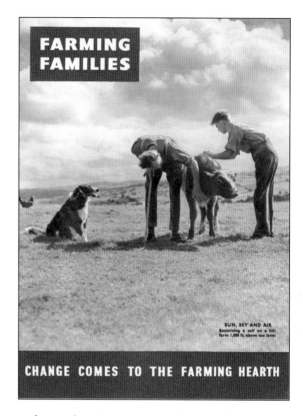

FARMING FAMILIES

SUN, SKY AND AIR
Examining a calf on a hill farm 1,000 ft. above sea level

CHANGE COMES TO THE FARMING HEARTH

of mechanisation at least of re-equipment'.

The introduction to the 20-page Aga pamphlet entitled *Farming Families*, reads:

> Today, homes which were built to be run by many pairs of hands have to be run by a few; often by the mistress of the house alone. In these new and more difficult conditions, the importance of the task has become no less. It is, in its

own way, essential maintenance – that of keeping the men of the house fit, fed and ready for work. Implements can be patched up and replaced, but human health and strength cannot be exchanged for new; the farmer and his family are irreplaceable.

And so, in the interest of the movement towards mechanisation in the field, we must not overlook the importance of labour-saving in the farmer's home. Since the earliest days of man, farmhouse life has centred round the fire – and usually round the kitchen fire. Generation after generation, through the centuries, the man came home from the fields to warm himself in front of the logs on the old, open hearth, while his wife heated the pot above the flames…for centuries the farming day began, and ended, in an atmosphere of

a cold kitchen and watched pots that would not boil.

Then came the range – massive in its dignity; ornate in its cast decorations, sleek in its blacklead. Oh! that blacklead and the endless task of keeping it clean… Fuel, too, was a perpetual headache; for, of course, big ranges had an appetite in proportion. You could put on a barrowload of coal and the range still came back for more.

Salvation came, of course, from the Aga, and the florid text from the typewriters of the advertising men at Mather & Crowther rose to the task of describing it:

In 1929 came a new form of cooker, the Aga, designed by a Swedish scientist. He had not, in fact, invented it specifically for the needs of the farmer; but in the results, he might well have done so… For the farmer is, in the nature of things, a

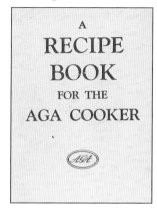

A recipe from the archives

The following recipe is taken from *A Recipe Book for the Aga Cooker*, published in 1945…

Queen of Puddings

Recipe: 2oz breadcrumbs, $\frac{1}{2}$pt milk, 1oz butter, grated rind of 1 lemon, 2 yolks of eggs, 1oz sugar, 2 tablespoons jam. Meringue: 2 whites of eggs, 3oz sugar.

Method: Bring the milk and butter to the boil on the boiling plate and pour over the breadcrumbs, add the sugar and lemon rind, cool slightly, add the yolks of eggs, and allow to soak for 30 minutes. Pour into the pie dish, stand in a half-size meat tin and hang on the middle set of runners in the roasting oven (or baking oven of the 4-Oven Cooker) until set.

Take out, cool slightly, and spread with jam. To make the Meringue: Beat the whites of eggs stiffly, fold in the sugar and pile on top of the pudding. Colour slightly at the top of the roasting oven for 2-3 minutes, and transfer to the simmering oven to set, at about 1 hour.

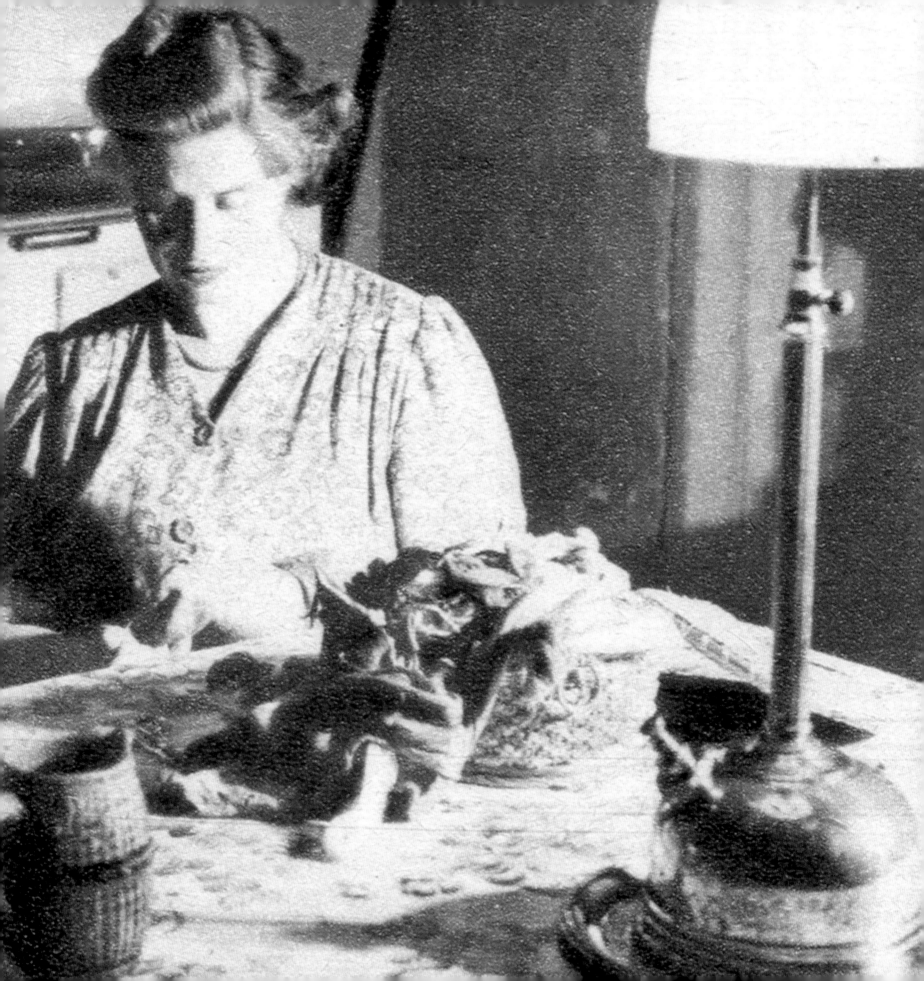

National heritage cast in iron

In 1947 Allied Ironfounders Ltd – owners of Aga Heat Ltd – opened its second manufacturing unit in Ketley, near Telford in Shropshire, where the famous range cookers are still made today. The following extracts from *The Story Behind a Symbol*, a pamphlet produced by the company to raise awareness of its work and its products, paints a fascinating portrait of an aspect of a group at the very heart of our industrial heritage…

'For practical purposes, British ironfounding began in the Midlands, in Tudor times; while modern methods were first developed at Coalbrookdale by Abraham Darby, in the years 1708 onwards. It was from Coalbrookdale that skilled men went forth, to set up the great ironfounding centres of Scotland. From these loins issued the modern light-casting industry.

'Coalbrookdale – a works of contrasts. Set in a beautiful Shropshire valley, spanned by the iron bridge which was one of the foundry's greatest achievements, and with the ruins of Darby's own furnace still there to see, for any who care to push their way through the wild flowers that surround it. And, on the same site, one of the most mechanised ironfounding plants in Britain still carries on the Coalbrookdale tradition – a mass of conveyors, cranes and complex handling equipment, for the

man whose movements cannot be decided by hours or timeclocks… It's no coincidence, therefore, that of recent years some of the most modern kitchens in the country – the kind of kitchens you see in exhibitions – have been installed on farms. And it's no coincidence that even in more ordinary ones you will also find the Aga, time after time. Look at it, if you like, as part of the progress of agriculture; as the country housewife's contribution to greater efficiency.

Among those profiled in the pamphlet was Philip Garrod, who still farms today with his son, Neil, at Little Blakenham near Ipswich in rural Suffolk. The mixed farm was chosen by Aga's advertising agency in 1949 because it 'seemed to us typical of life in an agricultural district in post-war Britain'.

Mr Garrod, now a young-at-heart 84, recalls the day when Aga sent a photo-journalist to capture images of life at Little Blakenham.

He stayed here a week. He stayed at the village pub because he was taking pictures of everything on the farm. He stayed at The Angel. He stayed here in the daytime, then went down the pub.

We were growing cereals and sugar beet, peas and beans. The main thing what we had then – because my father was alive then and he was a shepherd – was the sheep, you know, and we had to grow food for them you see. It was 283 acres then. We have 650 now.

Mr Garrod, whose late wife Ruby also featured in the Aga pamphlet, remains bitter at the way farmers, who were instructed by the post-war government to introduce intensive farming methods, are now seen as the villains of the piece.

'After the war I was an important man. Now we're not wanted at all,' he says.

But he has fond memories of the Aga which transformed life

at the farm...

I bought the Aga in 1947. I had to go to Cambridge to get a licence to have it. From the Ministry of Works. That's why this fellow wanted to come here because the Aga just stood in the kitchen – it wasn't fixed really – and there was a pipe went up the chimney and we had no water in the house, no electric light, nothing you see. And I had a tank in the back where you could pour water in, but you had to draw out the same amount straight away.

I had to get the licence from the Ministry of Works for the Aga. You had to do that for lots of things. I had to get a licence to build the new house. The Ministry brought up the chief executive officer to see where I was living. There was rats and mice running about and frogs and newts coming through the floor and they said a young man what's working as I was then can't live in these conditions with a wife and two children and with that I got a licence to build the new house.

Mr Garrod started work on the new house in 1950 and moved in – with his cream Model CB Aga – in 1952.

I bought the Aga from Warner's in Ipswich. It was Harry Warner what owned it then. Ours was a four-oven Aga. The Aga cost me five hundred quid. You don't forget something like that because then five hundred quid was a lot of money. I bought my first Ford car for a thousand pounds and that was years after then.

During the war I didn't work with my father; I went out on my own driving a threshing machine and bailer for local people and I saved a lot of money, as money was then. It don't sound much now, but I reckon if you took the value

Above: Mrs Garrod churning home-made butter and (top) Mr Garrod in 2002 at the age of 89

repetition production of castings in the quantities which the home and overseas markets now demand.

'…There is an art in casting iron – as in any other process by which the will of man is imposed, through the skill of his fingers, on to some insensitive material. And 'art' does not necessarily mean the filigree designs of early Coalbrookdale, or the lumpy realism of 'Stags at Bay', which stopped the doors of Victorian homes. Equally, it is there in the door of the modern cooker…whose smooth and silky streamline comes only of infinite care not only in the making of the casting itself, but in the enamelling and stoving which have replaced the traditional 'blacklead'. Of the men who work today each knows his job is a direct continuance of an established craft; knows too that in carrying it on, and developing it further, he is maintaining the standards which won for his grandfather the well deserved respect paid everywhere to a master craftsman.

'And therefore, in 1927, was formed the group known as Allied Ironfounders – an organisation which backed the specialist skill of the individual foundry with every resource needed for large scale development. The names and marks of the individual companies were already known throughout the world. Now is added to them the A.I. symbol – the hall-mark of modern British light ironfounding.'

of what I had then, that's more than I've got now. I wrote a cheque for the Aga. I have never borrowed a penny in my life.

Ruby was really looking forward to getting the Aga because we had an old Dutch oven. There was a hole in the side and the flames used to go through the side, you know. The first Aga was solid fuel. Ruby riddled it and filled it twice a day.

My wife worked as a housemaid at Shrubland Hall and they [the maids] used to have servants look after them in those days! There were scullery maids, kitchen maids. She was a housemaid and there used to be royalty from abroad and people like that come to stay at the hall and she had to look after them and the head housemaid had a car outside and a chauffeur to drive her round to get what they want!

There was an Aga at the

house where she worked and she wanted one. She liked the Aga. It was the first time we had had hot running water. [Before] if we wanted a bath we put an old bath up in one of the bedrooms and we had cold water put upstairs, you know, we put an old tank up there and a pump and we had to carry pans of hot water up there.

Mr Garrod, who decommissioned his old Aga in 1975 and replaced it with a blue, four-oven model, remembers how the kitchen was Ruby's territory.

She used to leave drinks on the top of the Aga for me and things like that, but I didn't cook on it or anything. I don't pretend that I did. Ruby used to do plain food, you would say. We used to live on meat and vegetables really. Nice fruit cakes and that sort of thing. I didn't have fillet steak or anything then.

I used to dry my gun on

the Aga – it was good for that – but I wasn't really allowed to go near the Aga. To tell you the truth, I wasn't allowed in the kitchen that much. That's the way we were.

But we kept everything then: pigs, chickens, sheep. We had the house cow that we used to milk. We made our own butter. We were nearly self-sufficient really.

Food rationing affected us less than most. Clothes rationing was the same, but we could get extra coupons for working clothes and for clothes for the workers on the farm. There were eight regulars on the farm and the War Agriculture Committee sent us help.

Only once did the farm play host to evacuees from London; their stay at Little Blakenham was a short one...

'A bloke who lived on another farm brought two ladies up here...They were evacu-

ated here with their three children, I think. They stayed one night and then they wanted to go back.

The night they went back that was pouring with rain when they were put back on the platform at Ipswich the crash warning had gone in London, but they went off like pigs running from a burning fire.

I was working until nearly midnight putting extra blackout material up and my wife was getting water for them and doing this and doing that, but they went the next night.

They wanted a fish and chip shop and a pub opposite!

The 1940s saw (top) a huge rise in installations of the Aga, while cookbooks of the time included handy hints for owners

1950-1959

Rise of the Agastocracy

For many, the fifties began with a spirit of optimism, a desire to cast off the drab war years

If the 1940s had been the decade of struggle – world war, the hardships of rationing and the long wait for things to get better – the 1950s were the years of colour. As if driven by a subconscious desire to cast off ten grey years of bully beef, Spam, clothing restrictions and endless making-do and mending, Britain in the 1950s emerged from its drab chrysalis as a beautiful butterfly determined to take to the skies in a riot of colour.

For most, standards of living increased dramatically and a national optimism replaced the 1940s' sense of resigned determination to get through. 'Isn't life colourful!' proclaimed an advertisement for Formica, the new worktop surface sweeping the land. 'Cooking's more fun in a gay kitchen,' read the headline to a similar advertisement for the new range of Alkathene houseware.

In her book, *Every Home Should Have One*, author Jan Boxshall describes the advent of the new decade and its effects on the British housewife.

The decade started in optimistic mood with the Festival of Britain in 1951, held on a transformed bomb-site on London's South Bank. Its 'Dome of Discovery' heralded a brighter future; the emphasis was on colour, fun and fantasy, in stark contrast to the austere war years.

One of the biggest crowd-pullers was the Home of the Future, featuring uncluttered rooms, electrical appliances galore and the new ideal for the 1950s housewife – a fitted

Early fifties advertising reflected the shortage and value of domestic staff in British households

kitchen. In the same year, a Mass Observation study found that the average British housewife worked a 75-hour week – spending about a quarter of her time in the kitchen. It wasn't surprising that women were crying out for new kitchens and more labour-saving gadgets.

By contrast, in the early years of the 1950s the marketing of the Aga was slow to respond to the changing mood of the nation. The message remained, essentially, the same. 'Change to an Aga cooker and water heater,' read an advertisement from March 1950, 'and enjoy its constant readiness, its immaculate cleanliness, its labour-saving, its tremendous savings in fuel, and all the hot water you need.'

In another campaign from May 1950, what was billed by Aga's advertising agency as 'a true and enchanting story' was used to sell the two-oven Model C with the tale of a new Aga owner in Surrey.

Mrs B, who is my very oblig-

ing domestic help, saved her earnings for years and bought an Aga. I didn't have one at first! And every day I'd hear 'Now, ma'am, if only you had an Aga'. At last my husband and I investigated. We discovered that the Aga does all the cooking and heats lashings of water…We changed to the Aga. We are so very glad we did.

Between 1951 and 1952, an Aga sales drive was conducted north of the border, with a significant publishing campaign launched to introduce Scots to the cooker doing so well in the south. In a 16-page pamphlet entitled *Your Home and the Aga*, no fewer than 17 Aga-owning Scots families were photographed at home with their pride-and-joy new cookers.

Mrs Paterson, of St Leonard's House in Ayr, believed having an Aga in the kitchen was akin to employing domestic staff. 'The Aga is as good as a resident maid,' she gushed. 'I can go out all the afternoon knowing food will cook safely in the simmering oven

A decade of innovation

Many of the innovations – technological and social – commonplace in Britain today made their debut in the booming 1950s.

The first supermarket (Premier) opened its doors in 1951, the same year Diners Club unveiled Britain's first credit card, while a year later Tetley introduced the teabag and the first telephone answering machine was launched. As early as 1954, IBM showcased what it called an 'electronic brain' – a forerunner of the computer.

In 1955, ITV made its first television broadcasts, as Wimpy – to become a common sight on British high streets – opened the first chain of burger bars. It was the decade of the first automatic electric kettle, our first taste of fish fingers, the Teflon-coated non-stick frying pan and the first time Britons were able to use Yellow Pages to locate a telephone number.

In 1958 the first-ever tumble drier went on sale and a year later Velcro was invented. The decade ended with the opening, in 1959, of the first stretch of the M1 motorway.

Facing page: images of fifties life at the home of Ian and Betty Gillespie of Stranraer

without supervision. And, in the morning, there is no fire lighting, no blackleading, breakfast is ready in 20 minutes and I have a cosy kitchen. And what a good cook the Aga is.'

Mrs Meldrum Smith, of Inverdovat, Newport, in Scotland, was lucky enough to have staff, but still found her Aga invaluable. 'With so little help in the house, it is essential. My maid, Margaret, can do all the cooking single-handed because the Aga is so easy to handle.'

Mrs M. Allen, whose family farmed in Keith, had installed a Model C Aga fitted with a six-gallon Aga Open Fire boiler. 'Hot water from the tank is so handy,' she said, 'for mixing calves' and chickens' food, for washing and for filling the tractor radiators in frosty weather.'

Mrs Betty Gillespie of Stranraer was featured heavily in the Scottish Aga sales brochure:

As soon as you step inside Claremont, Mrs Gillespie's delightful house, you can tell there is an Aga in the

kitchen. That's why there's warmth, there's peace, there's comfort all through the house.

And though the house was built before the servant problem, Mrs Gillespie now manages with little domestic help. "With the Aga in the kitchen I can cope almost single-handed," says Mrs Gillespie. "As we have so many visitors, often eight or nine to a meal, I need a cooker with plenty of room. The Aga gives me all I want."

Mrs Gillespie and her husband, Ian, had installed a Model E four-oven, three-hotplate Aga and an Agamatic boiler to provide constant hot water. Her only assistance in the kitchen came from Miss Murray who 'helps sometimes at Claremont. "The Aga is a joy to work with. The kitchen is always clean and so are the pots and pans".'

Mrs Gillespie's son, Iain, now 62 but still living at Claremont overlooking Loch Ryan, remembers the day the people from Aga came to photograph his mother and Miss Murray:

I was ten or eleven at the time and I was at school when they came. I think I probably wanted to stay at home, but was told to go. I remember our Border Terrier, Patsy, did get in the photographs – sitting next to the Aga and at my mother's feet while she did the ironing. My father brought her back from the war with him.

The Aga had been installed in 1949 by the Stranraer ironmongers James McHarrie. It was a Model E with a boiler and there weren't that many installed in Scotland at that time. But it is still here at Claremont and – though now converted to oil – it is still working perfectly. Even now, more than 50 years later, I like to sit on it with a wee dram and contemplate the world.

Mr Gillespie Jnr, a Master Baker at the family firm John Gillespie & Sons of Stranraer, said that the Miss Murray pictured in the pamphlet was a dear family friend.

'Mary had been my grandfather's housekeeper,' he said, 'from when his wife, my grandmother, died in 1936 and he retired. She was a lovely woman and very devoted.'

Shades of fashion

Such advertising campaigns painted an idyllic portrait of life with an Aga. Having been introduced some 20 years before, however, the Aga was starting to appear out of step with the demands of the modern British housewife. Despite having accumulated in excess of 50,000 sales with campaigns based on the virtues of economy and reliability, the Aga – paradoxically never a style purchase – was beginning to sound unfashionable. And the cream enamelling for which it was now renowned was beginning to seem out of sorts with the national desire for colour and lots of it.

Even with the obvious trend toward greater vitality and variety, the British public was to have to wait another seven years before the Aga entered into the spirit of the age with the introduction in the UK of the first-ever non-cream Aga.

Instead, Aga Heat Ltd began the

The Archers are at home with the range...

The Archers, BBC Radio 4's hugely popular 'everyday story of country folk', was first broadcast in 1950 and an Aga has been a feature of life in Ambridge almost since day one. An Aga was installed in the kitchen at Doris and Dan Archer's home at Brookfield and, when his son Phil with his wife Jill took over the farm, they inherited the beloved Aga too. Now Ruth and David are at Brookfield and the two-oven Aga, after almost five decades of service, has been given a new lease of life, with conversion from solid fuel to oil.

Authenticity has been a cornerstone of the success of the world's longest-running radio drama serial – which also features a Rayburn at Oliver Sterling's cottage at Grange Farm – and the production team behind *The Archers* has gone to extraordinary lengths to recreate for listeners the unique 'feel' of the Aga. In the 1970s, a cream two-oven Aga was installed inside *The Archers'* recording studio at the BBC in Birmingham so that 'spot effects' technicians could accurately record 'live' the sound of the Aga doors being opened and closed.

decade with the announcement of significant price increases. The news was broken on 30th April 1951 in a notice subsequently inserted into the pages of the company's newest brochure, presciently entitled *The Saga of the Aga*. 'Aga Heat Ltd announce with great regret,' the announcement to distributors read, 'an increase in prices of Domestic Cookers and Boilers.

'Despite the fact that costs have risen steeply during the past two years, the increase now announced is the first alteration in prices since 1947; and even now the average increase in the selling price of Aga products since 1939 is only 64 per cent.'

By 1951 – after some consolidation of the array of products manufactured in Smethwick and the new Ketley foundry – the Aga range comprised 14 products, five of them cookers: the Model C Cooker at £90; the CB (Plain) at £103.10s.; the CB (Bower Barffed) at £107.10s.; the CB (Copper) at £109.10s.; and the Model E at £122. The range was completed by four models of the Agamatic water heater (£45-£50),

two versions of the Aga Open Fire Boiler (£9.10s.), the six-gallon Water Tank for inclusion in the Model C or Model E cookers (£9.10s.) and a 30-gallon Side Tank for the Model C, available galvanised (£30) or in copper (£33).

Importantly, Aga now had a cohesive range of products. At its heart was the Model C 'for the average-sized household'. Still only available to run on solid fuel, the Model C featured twin hot-plates and two ovens and claims for its guaranteed annual fuel consumption had dropped to just two-and-half tons of coke, anthracite or Phurnacite.

The Model CB (the 'B' being Boiler) boasted all the features of the Model C with the added convenience of a built-in water heater. The Model E – forerunner of the modern four-oven Aga – was designed 'for the larger household… Four ovens and three hot-plates on top provide space for cooking large quantities of food'.

In each case, Aga promised what labour-saving virtues it could, notwithstanding the fact it was marketing a range of solid-fuel

The Aga iron is pressed into action

The 1950s saw the launch of 'an iron which needs no electricity, and which you can heat safely, simply and at no cost on your Aga Cooker'.

The beautifully simple cream-enamelled Aga iron, with black plastic handle and locking device and the script Aga logo, came in three sections: the cover and two sole plates.

The first sole-plate was heated on the Aga and then fixed to the iron. While this was being used, the second sole-plate could be heated ready to take over pressing responsibilities. 'The iron,' claimed the sales brochure, 'will retain heat for five minutes, ample time for the largest article...'

Aga Heat Ltd initially sold the Aga Iron by mail order at 37s 6d plus postage.

appliances: 'Just twice a day you need to add fuel, riddle the fire and clear ashes'. Not, perhaps, quite what many fifties housewives were hoping for. Still, however, the marketing men persevered: 'Life with an Aga is full of lovely discoveries big and little,' *The Saga of the Aga* proclaimed.

For instance, one day when there are breakfast sausages to fry, you'll tuck them into the roasting oven – and take them out later such a beautiful brown!

Then you'll let the roasting oven do all sorts of frying. Better results than ever before and no odours, no spitting fat to cope with!

And here are other instances of the bliss your Aga brings you. That front drying rail on the Aga, thanks to the constant fire, means quick drying for damp tea cloths and anything else you require in a hurry. And though the Aga will never let your kitchen become depressingly cold, it will

never make it unpleasantly hot – it is the considerate cooking companion in any climate, any season.

Some concessions to the *zeitgeist* of the early 1950s were being made. The Agas featured in brochures of the day were, for the first time, portrayed in the relative modernity of contemporary kitchen settings – and in glorious colour.

An architect, Mr Lawrence Wright, was commissioned to draw up plans showing the Model C and Model E as the centrepieces of two stylish kitchen conversion schemes. His drawings (previous pages and right) were based on plans conceived by Mrs M. Pleydell-Bouverie, similarly commissioned by Aga Heat Ltd.

The Model C was shown in a setting based on utilitarian pastels with details in red and blue-and-white candy-stripe wallpaper. Storage space abounded, there was a 'fixed table with seats for four persons', a free-standing refrigerator, room for a portable ironing board and a 'worktop with service hatch over and

A 'strange and unfamiliar contraption'

'Our first encounter with an Aga stove was in the mid-1950s, a few years after we were married. Both of us were serving RAF officers, but starting a home and a family led to my staying on in the service while my wife, Joanne, took on the vital job of providing the camp-following administrative support. We came face to face with what to us was a strange, unfamiliar kitchen contraption when, eventually, we moved into a pre-World War Two married quarter. During the 1920s and 1930s, the RAF, in its great wisdom, had installed Aga stoves in all its new officers' married quarters.

Our new-style cooker was a two-oven, solid-fuel affair and it took some time to become fully acquainted with it. At one time we had an American friend, with his large family, come to stay with us for six weeks while they found a suitable house of their own in the UK. He was a second-generation New York Italian immigrant and fancied himself as a great cook. Indeed, he did most of the family cooking (and often most of ours too).

When we first introduced him to the Aga, he was abruptly baffled, his eyes raising heavenwards as he discreetly crossed himself. Nevertheless he persevered and it

space for trolley under'. The Wright/Pleydell-Bouverie vision for the larger, four-oven Model E was a 'family kitchen/living room' in a small country house. With green-tiled flooring echoed by green work-top surfaces and complemented by natural wood fitted units, the kitchen boasted a host of modern features: 'double electric power point, broom cupboard, banquette with box under, strip lighting over, desk – sewing machine under, book shelves over, drop table, ironing board, back door – barn type, delivery hatch, dry store to ceiling, sink unit, dry store, pot rack and fly-proof window.'

Long-held advertising habits were, however, proving hard to break. Even as late as April 1955, the Aga was being marketed in a manner no different from the tactics adopted in the 1930s. Beneath the headline 'Ask any Aga owner', one advertisement from *Good Housekeeping* magazine saw Aga answering some commonly-asked questions… 'Can you bake cakes that are never "sad"?' asked one. 'Can you cook an egg-thickened sauce without "catching" it, ever?'

asked another. 'Can you cook ham, stock, porridge through the night?'

Elsewhere, it seemed as if the stiff, starch-pressed collars around the necks of the ad men were starting to loosen slightly. In a particularly witty advertisement from *Punch* the more relaxed attitudes of the day shone through. It began with the tag-line 'This is an advertisement' and continued…

There must be (we suppose) all kinds of rules that tell you how to put these things together. Somewhere among them it is sure to say that you must tell the reader everything that's good about your product. So let's do that, straight away, by numbers. It:- 1. Cooks like that legendary what's-'is-name; 2. Boils up water like billy-ho; 3. Burns day and night, and is as clean as a boy scout's whistle in thought, word and deed; 4. Is as much trouble as a genie with a lamp and saves your labour like one of those Indian affairs with eight hands;

Facing page: the Aga was promoted as being at the heart of fine living in the optimistic 50s

was not long before he was an expert and full of praise. In fact, when he left us he declared that if ever he were able to build his own home 'Stateside', he was going to fix it so that it had one of those Aga stoves.

When eventually we left the RAF we moved into a large farmhouse in Norfolk and promptly installed a four-oven, oil-fired Aga, which served us well for 20 years before we moved to smaller houses and installed two-oven models.

What will happen when the next 'posting' comes? Quite probably the final move. Surely there must be Agas in heaven. It's never quite been heaven on earth without one.'

JOHN MUSGRAVE, OF BURNHAM THORPE, KING'S LYNN, NORFOLK

A recipe from the archives
'We are enclosing your kind order for the *Aga Recipe Book* and in doing so we would like to apologise that there has been some delay over publication. It was hoped that the book would be ready rather earlier in the year, but unfortunately the Printing Trade dispute caused unforeseen delays. May we express the hope that the book will prove of

5. Uses a guaranteed bagatelle of fuel; and
6. Makes the owner feel dizzy with pride and the neighbours feel sick with envy. There! Not bad, eh?

The Aga's ability to expel cooking smells, keeping the kitchen free from unwanted odours, was not cited in that advertisement. For the young Sally Glazebrook it might not have helped anyway. As a young teenager in the mid-1950S, she was often left to cook for her father when her mother went out or had errands to run. On one occasion in 1955, things went horribly wrong at the family home at Pontruffydd Hall, Bodfari in Denbigh, Wales.

My mother left to go to a church meeting in the village. 'Put the tin of carrots in the Aga, heat them up and serve them with something,' she said. I duly put the tin in the Aga and retired to the sitting room with our old Retriever.

Ten minutes later it sounded like a bomb going off. The Aga oven door had blown off – the rail too. All the packing around the oven had blown out on to the ceiling with all the carrots too! The damage to all the kitchen was devastating.

I had not pierced the tin. Luckily, nor had I killed myself, my father or our dog, who loved to lie in front of the Aga.

The experience has not, however, dented Mrs Glazebrook's faith in the Aga. Now in her seventies and married for 45 years, she says 'I still have one and would never cook on anything else.'

Celebrating success
Any reluctance on the part of the Aga board to depart from a winning marketing formula is understandable. Between 1945 and 1950, 20,000 families switched to an Aga in the kitchen: a survey of new owners revealed that 54% had switched from gas and electricity and 46% from coal and oil. The Aga reputation was established, sales were healthy and owners old

real help to you.' So read a printed note inserted into copies of the *Aga Recipe Book* by the publishers, Wilding & Son Ltd, of Castle Street in Shrewsbury, when the book was finally produced – late – in 1956. The following recipe is taken from the book.

Chestnut Soup

Recipe: 1pt white or bone stock, $3/4$lb chestnuts, $1/2$oz butter or margarine, 1 heaped teaspoon cornflour, 1 gill milk, seasoning, pink colouring.

Method: Boil the chestnuts, after pricking them, for about 30 minutes. Peel off both outer and inner skins and chop the nuts roughly. Simmer the nuts in the stock with the seasoning on the simmering plate. When the chestnuts become pulpy, rub through a hair, or fine, wire sieve. Add the cornflour, blended with the milk, to the sieved soup and return to the rinsed pan. Bring to the boil, continue stirring and add the butter in small pieces. Cook for a minute or two, season again, if necessary, and add a few drops of carmine. Serve with fried croutons.

Facing page: in the fifties, the annual Aga dinners for its network of agents were lavish affairs. Inset: the menu for the 1957 event

and new were full of praise for the cooker that bucked the trend for gadgetry and technological innovation.

Arthur Price, who was Assistant Works Manager at Ketley, where the Aga was being made, looks back on the 1950s with excitement.

It was such a proud place to be. We considered ourselves to be the top of the league in the Allied Ironfounders' orbit. We were the bee's knees. We were pleased to be with Aga. We had a wonderful spirit.

We used to have a yearly conference and go to the Dorchester, and we had all the distributors invited and stayed overnight. It was absolutely fabulous being one of the younger members and not having seen a great deal of selling and advertising. The Aga was being advertised in the 'in' magazines of the day and it was never cheaply done; it was always done with style.

At one such conference – the 1950 seminar for Aga agents at the Dorchester Hotel in Park Lane, London – representatives of 112 UK distributors attended, as well as 25 agents from overseas, representing Aga outlets in the Republic of Ireland, South Africa, Kenya and Uganda, Australia, New Zealand, India, Pakistan, Malaya, Burma, Hong Kong, the West Indies, Ceylon, Cyprus, Malta and Canada. By 1950, then, it is clear the Aga reputation had spread far and wide.

Delegates at the 1957 conference, on 6th March at the same venue, were certainly looked after. Following toasts to the Queen (offered by Vincent Jobson, Chairman of Aga Heat Ltd), the company itself (by H. A. Warner, Managing Director of the Aga distributor H. Warner & Sons Ltd of Ipswich), the agents (by G. Saville, Managing Director of Allied Ironfounders Ltd) and the guests (by Charles Insch, MD of Aga Heat), the distributors enjoyed a lavish four-course dinner and were then entertained with a cabaret featuring 'the singing star

AGA AGENTS
CONFERENCE

DINNER

·

Dorchester Hotel
6th. March, 1957

Founded in history

In 1957 casting of the heavy floor mouldings for the Aga moved to the internationally renowned Coalbrookdale foundry in the Severn Valley. The Coalbrookdale Company was formed in 1709 by Abraham Darby. He chose Coalbrookdale because of its ample supplies of coal, iron, limestone and clay and good river transportation. In 1709, he discovered a way to increase production by smelting iron with coke (a modified form of coal) instead of charcoal and most historians identify this breakthrough as the beginning of the modern industrial age.

Throughout the 19th century, cast-iron fireplaces, ovens and stoves became a significant part of Coalbrookdale's output and it produced a complete line of solid-fuel appliances. However, the two world wars in the first half of the 20th century temporarily altered production and it wasn't until 1946 that the company was able to return to its more traditional products and produce a series of solid-fuel appliances, including the Rayburn.

In 1929, the Coalbrookdale Company became a subsidiary of Allied Ironfounders Limited which, in turn, was acquired by Glynwed in 1969. Today, the foundry supplies castings for the Aga and Rayburn and, in 2002, it once again produced a range of garden furniture first seen in the 19th century.

Tonia Bern and the world's fastest mind-reader Al Koran, television's sensational new star'.

'I feel wonderful about having played a role in the success of the Aga,' says Arthur Price, who remembers many Aga conferences with fondness.

> The Aga has achieved so much, from humble beginnings in a small foundry in Smethwick. It has become one of the diamonds in the pile.
>
> It is special because in its way it was a different way of cooking. You have to have an Aga and cook on one to appreciate it. It's a way of life. I have always said that AGA does not mean Aktiebolaget Gas Accumulator, where it originally comes from; it means A Great Achievement. And it makes me enormously proud of it.

The Aga could not, however, continue to resist the fashions of the age. Customers, advertising

executives, distributors, agents, sales staff and workers at the Ketley foundry all began to lobby for one of the most significant developments in the history of the Aga: the introduction of colour. For 34 years, the cooker had been available only in cream. Then, in 1956, a range of new colours was introduced.

The first colours to be unveiled were pale blue, pale green, grey and white, with black offered as an additional top-plate colour. With the exception of the grey – whose enamel never really took to Aga's high standards – the new hues were an instant hit with British consumers keen to brighten up their tired kitchens.

The early marketing attempted to reflect the mood of the nation with the unveiling of a new family of Agas – De Luxe versions of the Models C and E:

> Now – the brilliant new Aga in colours to match your kitchen. Just one splendid achievement after another. For now this magnificent new Aga, successor to a long

An Aga van passes the Balmoral estate on its daily round of sales and service visits

Start of a beautiful relationship

I remember 1952, when I started work for Allied Ironfounders at its London showroom at 28 Brook Street. I liked it there very much. It was the head office. The Aga was only one of the things we did, but it was the most popular and the best known.

During the war we were evacuated and my parents rented a house in Rake in Hampshire, which had an Aga; it was one of those with an internal water tank and a tap at the front for dispensing hot water. I was only a child of about eight, but I do remember my mother getting to know how to use it.

Then, when we moved back to London, she wanted one, so we bought one second-hand from an advertisement in *The Times*. It was a 47-10. When I started at Allied Ironfounders, I saw an Aga and said 'Do we make the Aga?' They said yes and it was then I realised I was in the right job.

HAZEL JORDAN, OF BEXLEY IN KENT, WHO WENT ON TO WORK FOR AGA FOR 50 YEARS

Cakes for tea at Claire's...

My first sighting of an Aga was in 1955. I was 16 and had travelled with a group of friends for a day out in the country at Parbold near Ormskirk in Cheshire. We missed the last bus back and, unable to find a public phone, I realised I'd have to use a private one to let

line of illustrious models, is made in five scintillating new colours. Brilliantly re-styled and with all the beloved characteristics that have made the Aga a domestic treasure, this incomparable cooker and water heater is designed to harmonise with today's kitchens. Even more exciting – the enamel on its top plate and front is impervious to all acids encountered in modern cooking.

For an extremely low deposit you can own one immediately in cream, green, blue, white or grey, or in combinations of any of these colours with black as an additional top-plate colour.

'Some colours are easy to do,' says Arthur Price, who was Managing Director at the Ketley site when the new hues were launched.

White, actually, was the first colour we introduced. The grey didn't take, so we didn't do that for very long.

It must have come from the sales side or from one or two of the agents. We used to have a yearly meeting in London with all the agents and they would have been looking round and seeing colours in kitchens. They would have said that we should be going into other colours as other kitchen appliances were. They saw Britain exploding into colours and kitchens changing.

The product development team at Aga took their inspiration from contemporary colour fashions, from magazines of the day, exhibitions and from consultants. The board at Ketley even pored over colour swatches in a brochure produced by Ford for its new range of cars.

But while the move to coloured Agas might now, with the benefit of hindsight, seem a significant development, the decision did not exercise the Aga management of

How to join the **AGA**stocracy*

Crowning glory—colour
Choose yours in cream, blue, grey, green, white, or in combinations of these colours with black as an extra top plate colour.

...and make life a bed of roses

those at home know I'd be late. I walked up this long drive with a tennis court on one side and a man gardening on the other, who kindly agreed to let me make my call. He led me into his enormous house and along to the pantry, with its bottled fruits, home-made pots of jam, and 'green' hams hanging from hooks on the ceiling. As I was using the phone there, I could see into the huge kitchen where a girl of about my age was washing up. On the opposite wall was this gigantic long piece of cream enamel which seemed to go on and on forever!

The following month I started a domestic science course at a local college. On our first morning we had to introduce ourselves, and guess who was in my class? Yes, Clare, the very girl I had seen washing up. From that day on, Clare and I became firm friends. I would visit her home most weekends... For tea there were always home-made cakes of every size and description, all made on the Aga by Clare's mother and her sisters. There was always such a wonderful atmosphere in the house that from then on I wanted an Aga of my own. My dream came true 17 years ago – a two-door 'baby' compared to the Aga in Clare's house, yet one that's so much a part of my family that it has moved home with me.'

JOANNE ROSE 61, OF HALE, ALTRINCHAM, CHESHIRE

the day. Two companies, Ecol and Ferro – enamel suppliers still used by Aga today – did much of the research work for the new colour options and, after only a brief discussion, the go-ahead was given.

'There was a board meeting,' confirms Arthur Price, 'at which, after much experimentation, we simply said "Yes, OK, we've got the yellow right now, so away we go".

In unveiling the new range of coloured Agas, the company also launched a new – short-lived – advertising slogan. Potential purchasers were invited to 'join the Agastocracy...and be comfortable, cosy and cossetted'.

The Agastocracy – registered as a trademark by Aga – was defined as being 'for one who puts up with only the best of everything'. And the price to join the Agastocracy? £135 cash or a deposit of £29.10s. and 48 monthly instalments of £3.0s.9d.

Aga made another change as the decade wound down. In 1958, it launched the smallest model yet: the short-lived Agathermic. Introduced in July of that year,

the two-oven cooker with an integral water heater was just 2-feet 11 inches wide and featured square cast-iron enamelled insulating lids and a single rectangular hot plate. It was additionally recognised by the Aga nameplate placed in the centre of the front plate panel above the ashpit door.

However, the Agathermic, available in white, cream, blue, grey and green, died young: it was withdrawn just nine years later.

Much more significant was the introduction of the De Luxe Model C and Model E. The cookers featured chrome-plated lid domes, replacing the former enamelled lids; a styled top-plate which was sloped to accommodate the handrail; a raised splashback; a thermostat control in the top left of the front plate; a larger ashpit door (each door of the Aga was now the same size); and a concealed flue chamber (for the first time hidden under an enamelled shroud).

In so doing, the research and development team at Ketley had created the design template for the style of Aga most in use today...

"*You know, dear, I think my Aga has been alight ever since the last Coronation.*"

1960-1969

Aga chameleon

When Prime Minister Harold Wilson told the nation that Britain's flourishing economy was being "fuelled by the white heat of technological revolution", he could, paradoxically, have been referring to the Aga, the range cooker that had remained largely unchanged for the past 40 years.

The sixties – with memories of the austere war years now distant and the boom of the fifties exceeded by yet higher standards of living and unprecedented consumer spending – were the Aga's golden years, a period of expansion and change and record sales figures.

It was the decade that saw the launch of the first oil-fired Aga; the unveiling, four years later, of the first gas-fired model; and the continued expansion of the range of colours available until, as the decade drew to a close, the prospective Aga purchaser could choose from a rainbow palette of no fewer than 10 vibrant hues.

With sixties Britain swinging to the backbeat of pop's exciting new sounds, the Aga was dancing in the glitterball sparkle of technicolour success!

The decade began, however, with a change that now represents a key indicator for Aga owners keen to date their cookers reliably. With Aga Heat Ltd now fully subsumed into Allied Ironfounders Ltd and a separate Domestic Appliance Division established and responsible for Aga sales, Divisional Sales Director Charles Insch (formerly Managing Director at Aga Heat) was compelled to issue a letter to all distributors from his office at Orchard House, in Orchard Street,

London W1 (telephone Mayfair 8454; telegrams Alifounder, Wesdo, London).

'We have been advised,' he wrote on September 15 1961, 'by our suppliers of enamel that owing to production difficulties it will no longer be possible for them to provide a coloured acid-resisting enamel to our quality standard.

'We are, however, able to obtain acid-resisting black enamel of the highest quality, and we therefore have to advise you that with effect from the 1st October all Aga and Agathermic cookers and Agamatic Model C boilers will be supplied with black top plates only.

'We would like our Agents to take the earliest possible opportunity of changing the top plates of their showroom cookers and Model C boilers; and in order to assist in this matter we will make a free exchange by allowing full credit on any coloured showroom top plates returned to Ketley Works after replacements have been fitted.'

This, though, was enforced window-dressing; greater changes were being planned. And so, as the Russian cosmonaut Yuri Gagarin made the first manned space flight and the contraceptive pill became generally available, the Aga entered a new phase and technicians within the company's Research and Development facility at Ketley began work on new ways of powering the solid-fuel range that had already notched up more than 30 years' service in British kitchens. The Aga was about to go multi-fuel.

The move to production of the first oil-fired domestic Aga cooker was, in fact, a long time coming. Back in 1959, Allied Ironfounders had launched two oil-fired versions of its Agamatic water boilers: the rather quaintly named OF30 and OF50.

'Wonderful news,' the British public was informed in an advertisement in November 1959's *Ideal Home* magazine, 'new oil-fired Agamatics arrive to set the pace!'

'Who's got an Agamatic?' it continued. 'House-proud folk who like things at their best, and who like things easy to run – and easy on the purse! And now, here's the best news on boilers you've heard for a

'Wonderful news,' the British public was informed in an advertisement in November 1959's *Ideal Home* magazine, 'new oil-fired Agamatics arrive to set the pace!

Who's got an Agamatic? House-proud folk who like things at their best and who like things easy to run – and easy on the purse!

And now, here's the best news on boilers you've heard for a long, long time. Now joining the Aga family are two new oil-fired Agamatic boilers.'

The campaign pictured left sold to sixties families the benefits of so-called 'packaged heating' and lashings of piping-hot water

A new decade, a new owner

As the 1960s drew to a close, the Aga found itself in new hands. In 1969, Allied Ironfounders Ltd's 40-year association with the cooker it had helped to become a household name ended when the business was acquired by Glynwed Ltd. Formed in 1939, Glynwed was originally a major metal manufacturing business.

The acquisition of Allied doubled the size of the business and, through Allied's substantial presence in the consumer products and foodservice markets, provided the basis for a radical transformation of its activities.

Over the coming 30 years, Glynwed was to sell its long-standing metal distribution, metal processing and building and foundry products divisions and focus on two core areas: pipe systems, producing UK brand names such as Durapipe and Viking-Johnson; and foodservice products, including the Aga.

In 1969, Gareth Davies (later Chairman of Glynwed) was elected to the board of the company as Finance Director shortly before the acquisition of Allied Ironfounders. 'I joined the board just before we did the deal, together with two other colleagues. Allied, which at that time was under a degree of financial strain, had been the subject of a hostile bid by another company.' Acquisition of the Aga brand was not, says Gareth Davies,

long, long time. Now joining the Aga family are two new oil-fired Agamatic boilers.'

The advertisement hinted at considerable time, effort and money having gone into researching the engineering behind the new fuel-supply option. 'Aga have been busy for years, experimenting and checking and checking again – an Aga oil-fired boiler simply had to be the best and most efficient anyone could find.'

Interestingly, the *Ideal Home* advertisement also included an Aga offer on what it called Packaged Heating. 'If you take your Agamatic as part of Packaged Heating, you get small-bore piping (easy and economical to install, no mess) and Agavector heaters ('Moving Air' heat for cosy health!)… Go on to Aga Packaged Heating – it's the future!'

The apparent delay in launching the first oil-fired domestic Aga seems – albeit with the benefit of hindsight – yet more remarkable when one considers that in 1959 Allied Ironfounders began manufacturing an oil-fuelled

version of its Heavy Duty range of professional cookers for use in canteens, hospitals and other large institutional kitchens.

A strong contender for the ugliest Aga ever produced, the six-feet wide beast with integral pan rack featured two ovens, each 22 inches wide and $31^3/_4$ inches deep, with a thermometer mounted in each door. It had a manually controlled, fan-assisted burner and a front-mounted control panel for oil, air and fan levels.

Early models (Aga ceased production after seven years) were fitted with an overriding thermostat mounted in the flue nozzle. The cooker ran on either 34-second Gas Oil or 28-seconds Kerosene.

When the oil-burning Model OB Aga did finally appear in 1964, its exterior appearance included two significant changes.

The first was the inclusion of two rectangular hotplates and insulating lids, similar to the earlier Agathermic model. The second – and another tell-tale sign for keen Aga-spotters – was the debut of the new Aga logo. Gone was the script Aga lettering contained within an now 72 and retired, the principal objective. 'The purchase of Allied was not seen then as a move to acquire the Aga business, but rather as part of a strategy to increase our presence within builders' merchants. The Aga was not regarded as the prize; indeed I don't think then that the Aga side of Allied was performing particularly well. I think it was the years after 1969 that the Aga really changed. It came to be the jewel in the crown as the years progressed.

'It all happened very quickly. I joined the board in the May and, by the end of August, the acquisition had been completed. Another company had made a hostile bid and we came in really as the white knight. It was pretty exciting; I was on holiday at the time and had to come back.

'We didn't particularly celebrate the acquisition. Rather, I think we tended to take it very seriously at the time. It was a big initiative to tackle something as big as that and I think we rather approached it with a degree of trepidation. We had always been a good performer, but I think the City was holding its breath to see how things turned out.'

oval; in its place, white, *sans-serif* letters on a black background, within a much smaller lozenge with squared-off ends.

Early marketing of the oil-fired Model OB sold it as the answer to the 'dream of every housewife who likes her cooking to be one-up on her neighbours'. Now the dream had come true…

'Joints miraculously succulent – unshrunk – never dried up. Hot plates and ovens ready for action 24 hours a day to give her a reputation for cooking no other cooker could possibly give her. Yet absolutely nothing to do – not even a dial to set. How's it done? This new Aga is *oil-fired*.'

The Model OB was not alone for very long. Its styling – very like a Rayburn – was soon developed further and, later in 1964, Allied Ironfounders unveiled a milestone model. Critically, the OC – an oil-fired Aga of the same styling as the solid-fuel De Luxe versions – was the first of the vintage models still manufactured today. Production of the OB, by contrast, ceased after only seven years.

By 1968, when the BBC made its first television broadcasts in colour, Aga followed suit and unveiled yet more colour options; the Model OC could be purchased in myriad hues: the cream, white, pale blue, pale green and grey available since 1956 were joined by four new choices reflecting the age – red, dark blue, black and yellow.

The technology within the Model OB's cast-iron shell revolved around a Don 6-inch vapourising burner – from 1995 manufactured by Aga itself – and a high/low-flame selection device attached to a thermostat pendulum or, later, an electric thermostat with a sensor in the roasting oven and a control panel positioned behind the outer burner door.

The OC was swiftly joined by the OCB with integral water boiler. Initially, British housewives were offered the OCB90, providing 90 gallons of hot water daily, joined, in May 1971, by the OCB135, supplying 135 gallons.

Finally, 1964 also saw the launch of the four-oven oil-fired Aga, the Model OE, and its water boiler sister model, the OEB.

There's a lifetime of grace and flavour in an Aga Cooker

The advantages of cooking with an Aga solid fuel Cooker are so numerous, so overwhelming, that we can only hint at them here. Aga treats food *tenderly*, cooks gently and evenly, preserving the full flavour and natural juices. (Succulent joints and baking in a class by itself). And, of course, an Aga Cooker heats your water too. Now there's a new Aga in the family . . . the brilliant automated *oil-fired* Aga (illustrated here). All the famed Aga benefits plus the effortless efficiency of automated oil-firing. Allied Ironfounders (who make Aga Cookers & Boilers) aim to make life *easier* and more luxurious for people. They ensure the reliability of all their products for the home and for industry. This singles out everything they make . . . VOGUE Baths for instance, LEISURE Cookers, Room Heaters, Sinks and Kitchens and RAYBURN Room Heaters. ALLIED Radiators too. So why not single some out for yourself?

Building on heritage

By this time, all Aga production had moved to the Ketley site near Telford in Shropshire, its sister foundry at Smethwick – where the cooker had been made for 25 years – ceasing production in 1957. The research and development department was the last to make the move across the West Midlands.

Arthur Price, Ketley Assistant Works Manager at the time and latterly Managing Director, says they were difficult times, with up to 150 workers at Smethwick losing their jobs when manufacture of the Aga there came to an end. They were, however, 'all treated well by Aga', he remembers.

We got involved with the Coalbrookdale Company, which was part of the group, and they'd got a big foundry down there, so we put all the floor moulding down at Coalbrookdale and my father came over and went to Coalbrookdale and ran the Aga floor-moulding foundry there. That was the first involvement of Coalbrookdale. The whole shooting match had been brought over from Smethwick and we took over the whole plant then.

I think that at Smethwick they were employing between 140 and 150. Some came across – a few, not many – but I think those who didn't come across were treated well. Foundry closures were part of the fabric of ironfounding. I think with the opening of Aga Ketley people at Smethwick regarded that as the beginning of the end.

Having said that it took 18 months, two years, before that happened. Research and development was left there when all the rest of the works had closed and it came across at a later date. They brought in the solid fuel to gas, to electric, plus the fact they were doing stuff other than Aga cookers – the boilers and fires.

A recipe from the archives

In a 1960s sales brochure entitled *The Many Blessings of an Aga Cooker*, the Aga Cooker Division of Allied Ironfounders Ltd offered the following recipe pictured below – clearly food photography has moved on somewhat since then!

Meringue Baskets
Ingredients:
3 egg whites,
6oz caster sugar,
6oz sweetened chestnut purée,
1oz melted chocolate,
$\frac{1}{4}$ pint double cream, 1-2 teaspoons brandy

Method: Whisk the egg whites until fairly stiff, then add half of the sugar and continue to whisk until the mixture will hold its shape. Fold in the remainder of the sugar gently. Place some rice paper or lightly oiled greaseproof paper on a baking sheet and draw four 3-inch circles. Spread a little of the meringue mixture on each circle and place the remaining mixture in a forcing bag fitted with a plain $\frac{1}{2}$-inch piping tube. Pipe three circles round each circle to form a basket shape.

Place in the simmering oven for about $\frac{3}{4}$ hour until firm. Turn the meringue baskets on their sides and leave in a warm place to dry through. The filling: mix together the chestnut purée, melted chocolate, cream and brandy, then spoon into the baskets.

Indeed the engineers and technicians in the new research and development facility at Ketley were to go on to make an enormous contribution to the success of the Aga in the sixties and beyond.

Originally in charge of R&D at the Smethwick works was Albert Morris. He, however, did not make the move to Ketley and his position as Technical Director was taken by Jim Simpkin, who died in the early 1990s. Phillip Cooper, who had joined the Smethwick works as a lab assistant after leaving school, worked with both men – latterly as Project Leader, a role which included development not only of the oil-fired Aga, but also the gas-fired model and, in 1975, the EL2 electric Aga.

Cooper, now retired but still living only a few miles from the Ketley works, remembers the mid-sixties as 'exciting times'. The department revolved around four sections: the research laboratory itself; the fitting shop; and two drawing offices, one majoring on Aga and Rayburn production issues and the other dedicated to new models. In all, 20 white-coated technicians were involved in the two pivotal launches of the 1960s.

'It was a time of great transition. Oil prices were dropping, I think, while prices for solid fuel were rising. We had seen the launch in 1959 of the oil-fired Heavy Duty Aga, but that was designed for commercial use and was not really a heat storage cooker in the truest sense. It was designed to heat up quickly for rapid response. Developing an oil-fired Aga for domestic use was a completely different challenge.'

Phillip Cooper remembers the real driver for change being a small number of companies unconnected with Allied Ironfounders who were exploiting the market for *in-situ* conversion of solid-fuel Agas to oil. While not inherently unsafe, the conversions did not meet Aga's exacting standards and they invariably led to the manufacturer's guarantee becoming invalid.

'These conversion specialists were working in the field converting the solid-fuel Agas, but the balance [the relative heat values of the simmering and roasting ovens, and the hotplates] just wasn't right. The conversions were also difficult to install and difficult to service, so we decided to make a purpose-built, oil-fired domestic Aga.'

Michael Warner, whose family had been Aga distributors in the eastern region since 1932, remembers how his father, Harry, played an important role in developing the oil-fired Aga. As Managing Director of Warners of Lion Street, Ipswich, he resolved to see for himself whether safe and robust conversion of a solid-fuel Aga was possible.

Mr Warner senior used the family's own solid-fuel Aga at home for his experiments and – despite his wife Anne's annoyance at seeing her beloved cooker being tampered with and regularly taken out of service – succeeded in achieving a satisfactory conversion.

His son, now 55 and no longer a director of Warner's, having in 1998 sold his stake in the firm which still bears the family name, recalls how the Model CB at home – purchased new only seven years earlier – became something akin to an ongoing laboratory test-bed...

It would have been the early sixties.
I remember I was doing my 'O' levels at the time. We had a solid-fuel Aga and my father got together with Don Engineering who were making vapourising burners for oil-fired boilers. He got them to provide him with some experimental burners because he was convinced the Aga could satisfactorily run on oil. He spent six months experimenting on the Aga at home. There were temperature gauges all over the place – in the ovens, on the top, everywhere – because he was taking four-hourly readings. My mother showed great forbearance. I don't remember any rows, more a gritting of teeth and a solid expression and endless questions about how much longer it was all going to take.

Anyway, my father succeeded in his experiment and he sent his findings in a report to Aga in Ketley. He told them: 'I've done it and here's the proof!'. In the early days, they didn't want to know really. Their view at the time was that the Aga was a solid-fuel range and they didn't want to be messing with it.

I think my father was quietly a little bitter when the oil-fired Aga was manufactured a few years later and went on to become extremely successful. He was also, though, willing to acknowledge that in the end it could only really have been done by Aga and Warner's, which in 1932 was, I think, the twelfth Aga distributor to be signed up, continued to distribute Agas.

And today – having successfully completed an Aga Foodservice Group training course and

*Object
of desire?
The distinctive
but short-lived
Agathermic*

secured his basic food hygiene certificate – Michael Warner is considering putting 28 years' worth of knowledge of the Aga to good use as one of the freelance team which regularly stages Aga demonstrations throughout the UK.

Phillip Cooper confirms that Don Engineering was recruited to work on the Model OB project. 'The oil-fired model would have to be serviced every six months, so we re-designed their burner so that it was easier to install and service.'

The Agathermic was used as the base design and prototype models were then field-tested. Often, this involved installation at the homes of senior members of the development team. They would then report back with their test results before final modifications were made, remembers Phillip Cooper.

'The OB was originally the Agathermic,' he says. 'which had bigger flue-ways to burn coal. The original solid-fuel Agas had smaller flues, meaning they had to burn a smokeless coal, either coke or anthracite. The Agathermic [pictured left] meant a much less radical re-design to make it oil-fired. But it was really with the OCBs and OE [launched later in 1964 with styling modelled on the De Luxe solid-fuel Agas] that we had an oil-fired Aga designed from scratch.'

Phillip Cooper recalls that the project went well. 'It was certainly a challenge, but I think it took only about six months and, in the end, it was fairly straightforward. It really didn't take that long once

the decision had been taken.'

The key dates of the mid-sixties support that view. The R&D team relocated from the Smethwick foundry to the plant at Ketley in June 1964. Before the year-end, British consumers had no fewer than five new models to choose from: the original OB; the two-oven OC and OCB; and the four-oven OE and OEB.

But the research technicians at Ketley were not done; they looked first at how the Aga might be insulated more effectively. In June 1966, in a memorandum to all authorised Aga distributors, J. Darby, Assistant Sales Manager at the Ketley works, asked that it be noted that 'from tomorrow [June 9], domestic model Aga solid fuel cookers will be supplied with vermiculite instead of keiselguhr for insulation.

'The procedure for packing with vermiculite is the same as for Aga oil-fired cookers and…all joints must be thoroughly sealed. Special care must be taken in fitting the ashpit rope and in sealing the ashpit tunnel and top oven heat conduction plate to prevent any air leakage into the fire unit.

'Four bags of vermiculite will be supplied with the Standard and De Luxe models and two bags with the Agathermic cooker.'

Then, in 1968 came the second major Aga innovation of the decade, when Allied Ironfounders – whose Aga Cooker Division was by this time headquartered in Cadbury Road, Sunbury-on-Thames in Middlesex – launched the first Aga to run on gas. 'We really didn't have to adapt the cooker much,' says Cooper, 'but what we did have to do was find a reliable gas burner. We had a lab in Manchester – the Aldenshall works, part of Allied – which was making gas-fired boilers. They designed the new burner.

'The other issue was that with oil there was no approval system to go through – no overall safety agency. That wasn't the case with gas. By then we needed the approval of the Gas Board. Fortunately, it laid down various tests that needed to be made and we were able to carry these out in the lab. The Aga gas cooker passed first time, as we knew it would.'

When Allied Ironfounders launched the new gas Aga – perhaps its most technologically advanced model –it did so with a dash of irony. A year before Man stepped down on the moon, advertisements for the latest member of the Aga family made the most of enduring simplicity.

> 'You've seen them,' the campaign entitled *The End of Cooking with Knobs On* began, 'We've all seen them. The sort of cooker that looks more like a Cape kennedy launching station than a cooker. Well, the new Gas Aga is different.
>
> 'It looks different. It cooks different. More tastily. More evenly. And it does many things that ordinary cookers don't. Like heating lots of water and having self-cleaning ovens and

hotplates. And the new Gas Aga doesn't have any knobs, because it stores heat all the time, sealing in all the juices, all the flavour, and making everything taste that little bit better. Aga cooking is real cooking. Even, all-over cooking. So now you can stop relying on the flasher flashing or the buzzer buzzing, you just know that everything will turn out delicious. Ask any Aga owner.'

Then – in an unusually amusing marketing initiative akin to the traditionally straight-laced Aga deciding to get up from its chair and dance with the times – the potential purchaser was offered five self-adhesive plastic knobs and dials. 'They're free from your Aga stockist and they don't do anything.'

And so – in the year Concorde made its maiden flight – the Aga was enjoying its most successful period in the four decades since it was first imported into Britain. As the swinging sixties drew to a close, it had a new proprietor (see panel, p110), its range of models was larger than ever before, was available in more colours than ever before, and was being bought in greater quantities than ever before…

Facing page: by the end of the 1960s, the Aga had truly entered the age of technology, with the launch of oil-fired and gas-powered models

NOW! OIL-FIRING COMES TO AGA COOKING!

AN AUTOMATED AGA. The dream of every housewife, who likes her cooking to be one-up on her neighbours and her water always piping hot. Now this has come true. Joints miraculously succulent—unshrunk—never dried up. Baking in a class by itself. Hot plates and ovens ready for action 24 hours a day to give her a reputation for cooking no other cooker could possibly give her. Yet absolutely nothing to do—not even a dial to set. How's it done? This new AGA is *oil-fired*. The cooking stays just as perfect because the inimitable AGA heat storage method remains the same. This method stores heat inside a thick insulat--ing jacket, controls it automatically and pipes it in just the right quant--ities to ovens and hot plates so that none is wasted. At the same time it uses some of the heat to provide hot water. Which means very low running costs.

An AGA needs only one control

1970-1979

Electrifying times

'People were looking for more colour in their lives. They preferred the new colours to the standard cream. We would have these demonstrations of the Aga over three nights of the week, perhaps twice a year. I remember how we would get up to 30 people come along. We filled the showroom; they were very popular.'
Aga distributor

After the heady days of the 1960s, Britain was brought down to earth with a resounding thud in the 1970s. The decade saw decimalisation, the first test-tube baby, the debut of the VHS video recorder and, in 1974, the opening of the first McDonald's restaurant. But it is most widely remembered as a turbulent time.

This was a period of power cuts, widespread industrial unrest, the three-day week, the television screen shrinking to a white dot at exactly 10.30pm and the 'Winter of Discontent' when rubbish was piled high in London's Leicester Square. Spiralling inflation led to male unemployment at a rate not seen since the 1930s and, with the decline in heavy industry, the expansion of the service sector saw growing numbers of women entering the workplace and, as a direct result, the advent of feminism.

There is little evidence in 1970s brochures for the Aga, however, that the movement was having a significant effect on thinking within the offices of Glynwed's advertising agency. 'The [Aga's] slow oven is perfect for keeping plates warm, or meals hot for tardy husbands,' reads one brochure.

Instead, sales literature continued to build on the Aga's reputation for solidity and simplicity. 'It puts cooking back a hundred years,' proudly proclaimed one deliberately ironic pamphlet from the early 1970s.

A century ago good cooks used a cast-iron oven. The advantage was the presence of an even,

Cats were a feature of several Aga brochures in the 1970s – a trend which was set to continue

all-round temperature that gave them complete control over their cooking. Something that even today's cookers can't guarantee.

At Aga, therefore, we endeavoured to put back the clock. Inside our cooker, you'll find a cast-iron oven that produces superlative cooking. It seals in all the juices. And all the flavour.

You'll also discover advantages that make it more than just a cooker. You get a piece of furniture that makes your kitchen warm and welcoming. You get gallons of hot water at little extra cost. You have a choice of fuel. And you can even add to the value of your home.

Norman Cook, founder of T. N. Cook Ltd, one of the longest-established Aga distributors, remembers the 1970s well. He set up the company in 1974 out of the ashes of Mason's, which had gone into voluntary liquidation after a proud association with Aga dating back to the early 1930s. Based then in Water Street in Skipton, Cook's quickly became successful.

The Water Street premises were an ex-fireplace merchant's. We employed about 14 people at the time because we also did central heating. We had a showroom with two or three Agas in it. One of them was always kept 'steaming' for demonstrations and so that people could see how it worked. We always tried to have the latest colours on show. That was important: it certainly spurred on sales a lot.

People were looking for more colour in their lives. They preferred the new colours to the standard cream. We would have these demonstrations of the Aga over three nights of the week, perhaps twice a year. I remember how we would get up to 30 people come along. We filled the showroom; they were very popular.

There was Ray Moore – he was an engineer – and Bill

Elliman, from Halifax, the regional sales representative. He was very theatrical. He would do all the talking before the demonstration and all the talking afterwards. It was a lovely affair. We had tea and biscuits and everyone really enjoyed the evening. Some people used to come several times just because they had a good time!

The cooking was done by the demonstrator. Initially she was supplied by Aga. Later, we took on our own. She would always do something like a big fruit cake – which was ceremoniously handed round at the end – a joint, a Yorkshire pudding and lots of buns. They were very successful events.

T. N. Cook Ltd, which expanded in 1999 into larger premises on the outskirts of Skipton where the company now showcases 'Agas in every colour – I don't think anyone else has that', was set ambitious sales targets by Glynwed.

'We were supposed to sell 50 cookers a year,' says Norman Cook, now Company Secretary of the firm in which his son, daughter-in-law and grandsons are still involved.

But in the 1970s we were selling 75 or so, sometimes more. I think at one time there was this target sheet at Aga and we were in fifth place nationally.

I don't think we felt the unemployment of the time too hard here. The strikes and the power cuts didn't affect sales a lot really. I think that in a time of stress, people look for value for money and that's what the Aga offered. Yes, it was expensive, but it paid for itself.

One thing I did notice was how the customers changed: we were putting Agas into small terraced houses in town, whereas before it had been a country thing.

Hazel Jordan, who can celebrate a 50-year association with Aga and

back to the house to meet us some years later, together with a television film crew making a story of his life. He was astounded to see the Aga back in full working order, although new lids had by then replaced those which were somewhat dented when he threw them out!'
PAULINE TORODE OF GUERNSEY

My Aga memories
'The gentleman standing by his Aga van is my uncle, William Sizer.

When the war ended, he became an Aga engineer for a Hull-based company. By the time of his retirement in the 1970s, he reckoned to have installed 990 Aga cookers, regretting that he never finally managed 1,000.'

RICHARD SIZER OF FARNBOROUGH, HAMPSHIRE

Recipe from the archives
If you take your cooking seriously, you must have a clean dishcloth. The following recipe is very good for country people who don't want to send bleach or strong stuff into their septic tanks…

Ingredients: 1 dirty dishcloth or handkerchief, 1 dessertspoon washing powder.

Method: Place the dishcloth and/or

who, despite retirement, is still an Aga demonstrator, joined Allied Ironfounders in 1952 as a showroom assistant in London before moving to Glynwed's head office in New Coventry Road in Birmingham in the early 1970s.

In 1977, she became an Aga representative, charged with the job of liaising with distributors in the south-east of England, in East Anglia and, up the right-hand side of the country, as far north as York. Her lively reminiscences include the power cut that threw Charing Cross station into near darkness, and the Aga 'dem' in Lincoln where one of the audience told her she 'would rather have an Aga than a man' – her logic being that 'it's always warm and no "aggro".'

In her charming book, *A Lifetime of Aga: Recipes and Recollections* (self-published, 1997), Hazel Jordan also remembers one of the 'pioneers of the Aga' in the UK.

Ida Grove told me how she used to go round in a trailer with a working solid-fuel Aga, knocking on doors and offering to cook dinner for

the householders… Ida was one of the demonstrators whose job was often to visit a customer in her own home to show how to use the cooker. Approaching cooks in the kitchens of large country houses was not always easy, as it was necessary to ask the cook to alter her normal methods. To persuade women who had perhaps been cooking on open ranges to adjust to a thermostatically controlled cooker was a job requiring much tact, particularly when it came to insisting that the insulating covers must be kept down when the hotplates were not in use.

The Aga offices were in London – Orchard House, next to Selfridges. Although part of the Allied Ironfounders group, they were very much self-contained, with a showroom in North Audley Street and a staff canteen in the basement. There was also a training school for the handkerchief in an old pan. Cover with water and add the washing powder. Bring to the boil (don't allow it to over-boil) and leave in the simmering oven for as long as possible (you will be horrified at the colour of the water). Rinse several times until the water is clean.'

CLAIRE BUDENBERG OF LOWER WITHINGTON IN CHESHIRE

Pam Ayres' ode to a friend

'If the house is full of people waiting for me to turn out something stupendous, you'll find me running round the Aga in a blind panic trying to time everything and getting nowhere. I face thousands of people all the time when I'm working or touring. We prefer to be at home the rest of the time, just us, the kids and a home-made pizza.

'I love the Aga. It really is a family friend, I feel very affectionate towards it. It is always there when you need it. I have it on all year round. People come into the kitchen and automatically lounge against it. It is a warm focal point.

'And the dog and I always sit with our backs against it. Lovely! The drying rack over it has seen some history – drying all my sons' clothes, from tiny baby bits to huge rugby shirts! And when we tried our hand at farming, with a herd of 50 sheep, it saved the life of a lamb. It was weak and dying and we put

salesmen (and they were always men in those days) in Portman Mews South.

Looking back on the 1970s, Hazel Jordan does so with 'great fondness':

I remember how we had to wear uniforms in the showroom. In the winter we wore a plain, fitted dress in navy blue, with three-quarter sleeves and a pleated skirt. Then there was a yellow uniform – not at all horrid. A nice yellow dress with a jacket.

I remember the people most. Kenneth More, the actor who played Douglas Bader in the film *Reach for the Sky*, came in with his wife to see the Agas on display. He was such a charming fellow. He came in and, like many actors, seemed to be able to put people at ease. He made me feel so comfortable. He bought a bright red, four-oven Aga, but I seem to

recall that when he actually got it, at home, he decided it was a bit much and he opted for black instead.

We would have Americans come into the showroom in Brook Street – Claridge's was just down the road – and they would say, 'Excuse me, but what is that thing?!' I remember the new colours – we had about four of them, [including] a black one, a green one in the showrooms, and they were certainly very eye-catching.

We had a visit from Princess Margaret and Anthony Armstrong-Jones, but I remember the distributors most. They were the unsung heroes of the Aga story, I think.

Hazel Jordan is herself remembered by distributors. John Kirkham, Managing Director of A. Bell & Company, of Northampton, says she was known to all as 'Mrs Aga' and he jokes that 'I'm sure that if she were cut in half, she would have the word

it in the bottom oven of the Aga and it brought it back to life.

'I also dry herbs, flowers and kidney beans in it, iron my tea towels on it and raise yeast for bread in it. Without the Aga I'd be raising yeast in the airing cupboard and cranking up the oven to the right temperature every time I wanted to make dinner. I don't know what I'd do without it.'

PAM AYRES, THE COTSWOLDS

Thirty one and going strong
'We bought our Aga late in 1971. We had just moved to Norfolk and, once the farmhouse had been renovated, we bought a four-oven, oil-fired Aga from C.T. Baker of Holt.

'The wide array of colours on offer in those days was of no great importance to us: it had to be white and I seem to remember we ordered it over the telephone.

'As a family, we had had a long association with Agas. My parents had a four-oven Aga and my wife Ann's grandparents had an Aga. When we married and set up home in Suffolk in 1965, Ann's grandmother said we simply had to have an Aga and she gave us a four-oven white model – one of the first oil-fired models – from Warner's of Ipswich. Anyway, when we moved to the farm here in Edgefield – where we have been hobby farmers ever since and now have nine acres and seven cows – we

Aga written through her. Everyone who worked with her remembers her with the greatest of affection.'

The management team at Bell's spent much of the late 1970s engaged in negotiations with Glynwed, the Aga's new owner, to become an official distributor. The firm, established in 1889, had been an Esse retailer but was seeing sales decline. The Aga – with its attendant image as a lifestyle purchase – offered greater opportunities. John Kirkham notes:

> People were asking for the Aga and there seemed to be little commitment behind the Esse. I may be wrong, but I think it was in the 1970s that the Aga first began to outdo the Esse. It was then that it started to establish itself as something more than just a cooker – something closer to how it is perceived today, what it represents today.
>
> I'm from a farming family. As I grew up in the 1950s people either had an Aga or an Esse, but in the 1970s it

seemed to me that, as far as consumers were concerned, the Aga became known as something very special. I think it is the softness of the design, coupled with the fact that it is always warm. These two things create for the British, I think, a homeliness and a feeling of well-being, of reassurance.

> It is not easy to put into words, but in the 1970s what sticks in my mind is how most kitchen appliances were being manufactured to price; to be a pound cheaper than their competitors and the quality was secondary. The Aga bucked this trend. They said that they were not going to cut back on the quality of the product.

Mr Kirkham believes the Aga's inherent solidity was a key selling point. He cites with relish how one well-known manufacturer of more conventional cookers launched a competition to find the oldest of its products still in working order. The

knew we had to have an Aga and that it had to be white to replace the one we had left behind in Suffolk. And now, 31 years later, it's still here and going strong.'

RICHARD BROOKS, 61, OF EDGEFIELD, NORFOLK

Why do good cooks love the Aga?

And why do people who thought they weren't good cooks, suddenly discover they are?

winning cooker was around 20 years old. 'The Aga by contrast,' he says, 'is such a permanent thing: there are countless Agas from the 1940s and 1950s, some from the 1930s, still merrily chugging away!'

John Kirkham also recalls how the troubled times impacted on business at Bell's, which today sells around a hundred Agas a year.

> We were also Calor Gas retailers and we were incredibly busy. I remember getting into work one morning at 7.30 and there being a queue of 20 people waiting outside trying to get Calor Gas because of the fear of power cuts. We also sold many water containers because of rumours that there was going to be a water shortage.
>
> The other thing we noticed was that, whereas even in the 1960s men were the decision-makers – even on matters such as sinks – in the 1970s there was a big difference: women were increasingly making the decisions and if we hoped to make a sale, then it was the woman of the household who, very often, we had to impress. That was a dramatic change.

The business of change

When compared to the decades that had preceded it, the 1970s was a relatively quiet time for the Aga in terms of new developments. After the heady days of the introduction of oil-fired and gas-fired models, it was to be a further seven years before Aga was to bring something significantly new to the market.

Terry O'Neill, a former Chief Executive of Glynwed's Consumer Products Division, was brought in to restructure the business. He offers an interesting perspective on why a protracted period of calm followed the marketing storm of the exciting new model launches.

'Glynwed did nothing with the Allied Ironfounders business for years,' he says. 'It was moribund but, having bought it, nothing much

was done with it. After about four years, Glynwed did have some idea that its acquisition was not being developed. But the board, then, was what the City would have called "a bunch of West Midlands metal-bashers". It was the distributors who pushed for change.'

In the Aga, Glynwed did not really know what it had, according to O'Neill. 'It was like the Green Party,' he says. 'Not many people knew it, but those who did know it knew what it stood for. The Aga at that time was a little like those perfect holiday destinations we've all been to, but keep secret for fear of others spoiling it. We decided to protect its reputation.'

From 1977, O'Neill was charged with the job of adding structure to the disparate elements of the businesses inherited with the Allied acquisition. He took the six key elements – Vogue baths in Bilston, Flavell cookers in Leamington Spa, Falcon catering supplies in Falkirk, Leisure cookers in Long Eaton, the Rayburn and the Aga – and put in place management teams covering sales, financial planning and strategy and operations.

By 1982, Allied's 'significant losses' had been turned around and the Glynwed division reported an £18m profit.

Much of that success, he says, was down to some key members of the management team at Ketley. He singled out for praise Arthur Price, former Managing Director at the works, and Alan Bishop, his successor and now Managing Director, Operations, within the Aga Foodservice Group. 'They made the Aga. They lived and breathed it.'

Perhaps a little oddly – considering the fashions of the day – the decade began for the Aga with Glynwed deciding on the withdrawal of two colours: the yellow and pale green options. These were to be followed, four years later, with the deletion of grey, pale blue and black from the Aga palette of colour options. Then, in 1978, black was re-introduced as a colour for Aga fronts.

The first – and only – new model launch of the decade came in 1975 with the arrival of the EL2 (pictured right). The two-oven electric cooker, launched in the November of that year, represented a radical departure for Glynwed and its Aga business. Its styling was different from any Aga that had preceded it, lending it an appearance closer to the conventional electric cooker of the day.

Not clothed in the familiar, trademark cast iron, the EL2 was made from sheet metal and was available during its short life in some truly remarkable colour options: while the base cooker was white, prospective purchasers could opt for the splashback section to be delivered in white, red, dark blue, green, orange or chocolate. A sign of the times indeed.

The EL2, though never heavily promoted, was marketed to the British consumer as The Electric Aga. 'When we sold our first Aga,' read the sales

brochures of the time, 'frankly the choice was pretty limited: one model, one colour, one fuel. Today, things are rather different. A choice of models, of colours and of fuels: oil, gas, solid fuel and now electricity. Indeed the only thing that hasn't changed is the Aga reputation for reliability.'

Sadly, however, the EL2 could not match the legendary reliability for which its predecessors had become famous and the model was withdrawn from production after just two years. It was to be a further eight years before Glynwed returned to the market with another electric Aga.

The EL2 was fitted with a ferrous oxide heater core with 16 ceramic-housed heating elements totalling 6kw at 240 volts. The ovens vented into the overhead hood with the appliance's controls mounted on the attached fascia. It was designed to draw electricity overnight, at nominal charge, during the eight hours of off-peak usage.

'Overnight,' read the brochure, 'when electricity is cheaper, it builds a reserve. During the day it calls on this reserve to give superb, day-long cooking.'

Phillip Cooper, Project Leader at the time within Glynwed's R&D facility at the Ketley works, remembers poor element quality being at the heart of the short-lived EL2's problems.

'There were four banks of elements designed to take electricity off-peak for about eight hours each night, I think it was then, so that the core could be built up ready for use through the following day.

'If one element went down, then the 6kw needed was reduced to four-and-a-half. It also made the cooker more expensive to run.'

In all, just two hundred or so EL2s were sold during its three years of availability and the decision to cease production had more to do with its sales performance than its inherent 'un-Aga' feel. 'We used to say here,' said one senior Aga executive, 'that it wasn't really an Aga. It just didn't look right and I think it was withdrawn for that reason really.'

Disappointing sales of the EL2 did nothing, however, to dent Aga's reputation and, as the recession-ravaged 1970s gave way to the conspicuous consumerism of the 1980s, sales of the more traditional models were continuing to grow and Aga was making preparations for a period of unprecedented success...

Facing page: despite its distinctly thirties feel, this image was used in the seventies to underline the Aga's legendary durability

1980-1989

Conspicuous consumption

'Just ponder, for a moment, the changes in the kitchen seen through the eyes of an Aga…the cooks and maids have all but disappeared; the open fire in the kitchen is no more; we're into the built-in era for sinks and cookers; there are things like liquidisers, deep-fat fryers and mixers, even, heaven help us, electric can-openers'

Like those of a gracious lady of a certain age, the Aga's official birthdays have sometimes been clouded in a degree of confusion. So when Glynwed celebrated the Aga's fiftieth birthday as the first year of the 1980s drew to a close, the timing might seem a little odd.

Fifty years from the date of the cooker's invention would have been 1972; fifty years on from its first importation to Great Britain would have been 1979; fifty years from the date of its first manufacture in the UK would have been 1982. Interestingly, Glynwed was to celebrate its own fiftieth birthday – and 60 years of the Aga – in 1989.

Whatever might have been the correct date, the Aga's official golden jubilee occasion was marked with a lavish conference and dinner on 6th November 1980. Staff, distributors, demonstrators, technicians and management executives gathered at London's Royal Garden Hotel to be entertained by Michael Bentine, former star of *The Goons*, and the very same David Ogilvy, who, in the 1930s, had been Aga's first Scottish sales representative.

In the winter 1980-81 edition of *Aga Cooker News*, a 'quarterly bulletin for Authorised Aga Distributors', an unsigned editorial comment entitled 'The Next 50 Years: The Message is Still the Same' urged all those involved with the Aga to enjoy the moment, but not to lose sight of the challenges that lay ahead.

'Certainly,' the author writes, 'the November Conference and Dinner in London was an appropriate way to end the first 50 years, but we

As the Aga entered the eighties, advertising continued to focus on the 'modern housewife'

must not just move into the fifty-first year without some lessons from the past being learned.' What followed predicted, in microcosm, the themes of this book.

What have we to show for 50 years' dedicated selling of such a unique product? The most obvious answer is to be seen in thousands of kitchens throughout the land. Just ponder, for a moment, the changes in the kitchen seen through the eyes of an Aga over this time: the cooks and maids have all but disappeared; the open fire in the kitchen is no more; electricity is now a vital element in all kitchens; we're into the built-in era for sinks and cookers; there are things like liquidisers, deep-fat fryers and mixers, even, heaven help us, electric can-openers.

When the Aga first saw the kitchen, refrigerators were virtually unknown, domestic freezers were 30 years away, and the wooden spoon was the most widely used kitchen implement.

Yet through all these changes, and the many more that spring to mind, the Aga is the only thing that has survived – and not just survived, but increased in value, acceptability, usefulness, economy and even fashion.

The Aga is to be seen frequently on television in 'up-market' homes. Aga cookers are in daily use throughout the top households in the country. In a few words – the Aga has been established as the best.

The rallying cry went on to urge all those involved in the manufacture and selling of the cooker to make quality and innovation their bywords.

In the next 50 years, we, and those who follow, will have to ensure that this reputation is maintained, and even enhanced.

No doubt the product

Guest of honour at the Aga Jubilee Dinner in 1980 – held at the Royal Garden Hotel in London on November 6 – was David Ogilvy. A souvenir edition of *Aga Cooker News*, the quarterly bulletin for authorised distributors, paid tribute to him in suitably colourful fashion.

'David Ogilvy, who travelled from his home in France to be with us for the evening ... went to great lengths to say how delighted he was to have been asked to attend.

'In his after-dinner speech, David regaled the audience with some of his most frantic moments as a junior chef before he went on to become Chairman of one of the world's largest advertising agencies. It was an honour for the Aga that this great man was willing to come to London just to partake in our celebrations.'

Further after-dinner entertainment at the Jubilee celebrations was provided by former Goon Michael Bentine who 'with a varied and improbable assortment of props kept the guests entertained for an hour. The theme of his talk was 'My Life with the Aga' – although what the Aga had to do with some of his stories was obtuse to say the least!'

Facing page: the Aga's unique styling and signature enamelling have proven to be enduringly popular

itself will change – hopefully we will see an electric Aga one day, and even (as Kenny Everett would have us believe) a nuclear-powered Aga!

The Aga still has a great future; it is up to all of us to ensure that the next 50 years are as successful as the last.

Ahead of its time

In fact, a further five years were to elapse before the arrival of the first true electric Aga, the two-oven EC2. It was followed two years later in 1987 by the four-oven version, the EC4. Both are still made today.

Early advertising of the electric Aga – and, unlike the earlier EL2, these new models were clothed in the traditional cast iron – described it as an 'achievement of modern technology, yet one which delivers all the traditional Aga virtues and qualities'.

The new Aga was indeed radically different from its competitors. The 1987 brochure, entitled 'The Tradition Continues. The Range Extends', continues: 'The two-oven or four-oven Electric Aga is, naturally, quite unlike any

other electric cooker. The Electric Aga is the only cooker in the world that uses overnight, cheap-rate, Economy 7 electricity to cook with during the day. It cooks food like no other cooker can and while doing so it cheerfully warms the kitchen as well.'

Available from the outset in blue, red, green, brown, black, white and the omnipresent cream, the biggest changes to the new Aga were beneath its glossy, enamelled skin. The EC2 and EC4 had no internal burner: instead, a ferrous oxide heater core boasted 14 ceramic-housed elements totalling 6kw at 240 volts. Both hotplates and the top oven were heated by hot air forced through the heater core by a fan. No conventional flue was required as the electric Aga was vented by a small fan piped to the outside. The first models featured a control panel usually mounted on the wall adjacent to the Aga itself.

This panel included a clock and minute minder. In 1990 some modifications were made: the control panel moved to become integral to the cooker (without the clock and timer) and the oven vent fan was changed to allow fixing on

A recurring theme in Jilly Cooper's novels

As well as gorgeous, badly behaved people, fabulous houses and adorable animals, the Aga also features in most of Jilly Cooper's books and, of course, in her own kitchen.

The kitchen – which her husband, Leo, describes as 'the engine room of the house' – is exactly as one would imagine it: a large, scrubbed-pine table takes centre stage and a navy blue Aga the size of a small car is surrounded by tiles illustrating an idyllic country scene.

'There's an Aga in *Pandora*,' says Jilly, 'Rosemary has a lovely new kitchen and everyone comes to look at it. And Taggie cooks on an Aga. There are masses of Agas in my books. You know people just don't seem to get together to eat as a family anymore, but I think the Aga does pull people in, keep families together. I love it because although we have a large house, we're always in here [the kitchen] and we wouldn't be if it weren't for the Aga.

'Bessie [the Coopers' Labrador] loves it and of course it's very nice if you have an animal who isn't well – they can sleep in baskets by the Aga and always get better. It's a member of the family really. Though when we first got one, we couldn't get it to work and it was known as the "Aga Can't"!'

JILLY COOPER (PICTURED RIGHT), GLOUCESTERSHIRE

an outside wall.

The electric Aga was, as its associated advertising campaigns claimed, a significant step forward in heat storage technology. The cooker, however, was initially beset by problems. Despite Aga's best efforts to find robust enough heater elements to meet the demands of a cooker running 24 hours a day, seven days a week, the crucial parts in early models proved unreliable.

Jonathan Cooper, proprietor of Cast Iron Cookers in Norfolk, began his 20-year career as a service engineer just two years before the introduction of the EC2. The new electric Aga was, he says, to prove a baptism of fire.

> When you live with an Aga, cooking is a small part of it. Every single week I get somebody say to me that if it goes out – perhaps if they run out of oil, for example – it's like a death in the family. Nothing runs like an Aga – 24 hours a day every day from the moment it's lit. Most central heating boilers would work, what, six hours a day maximum.
>
> All the breakdowns on the electric Aga were components not made by Aga. When we put a new Aga in we build it properly to get it right for the customer. We would light it and know we would not see the customer again for another six months, when the Aga would be due for a service.
>
> With the electric Aga, I would be getting home at midnight – or later – every night because everything had to be right. We were working every day for months. We would do everything right, everything as it should be, but we just knew it was going to break down.

Jonathan Cooper, who has built up a customer base of more than 750 Aga and Rayburn owners, was at pains to stress that blame for the inherent problems with the early-model EC2s should not be placed

When Thatcher saw red

In 1981 Margaret Thatcher visited Glynwed's works at Ketley in the West Midlands amid high security. After being introduced to workers and senior management and escorted round the site, the Prime Minister was shown a brand new blue Aga. 'It's a lovely colour,' she said, a smile hinting at pride in the Aga's apparent political allegiance. 'It was red yesterday!' countered Glynwed's Chairman to much laughter.

Now you see it...

'We once installed a new 4-oven oil Aga where there was an old solid-fuel one. It was at a children's home in Suffolk. There was this old boy lived there – I think his grand-daughter ran the home. Everyone called him Grandad. He always used to come into the kitchen and lean on the Aga. We went there one day and took out the old Aga, but it was quite a bit of work to take it out so we didn't get actually get to start work on putting in the new one. Apparently the old boy came in that night and, because his eyesight wasn't what it once was, went to lean on the Aga that was no longer there. He ended up in a heap in the hearth where the Aga used to be!'

JONATHAN COOPER, SERVICE ENGINEER, BACONSTHORPE, NORFOLK

at Glynwed's door. 'Aga did everything they could,' he says, 'to find elements that were up to the job. They didn't want to see the elements failing. An Aga is a lifetime purchase and the electric Aga was really the only hiccup in 80 years.'

Alan Bishop, who became Managing Director of Glynwed's Aga operation at Ketley in 1989, makes the point that the electric Aga was ahead of its time. 'We were at the leading edge of technology. There were night-storage heaters, but there was nothing like the electric Aga.'

He explained how the R&D team at Ketley established that there was a point at which the heat being drawn into the elements within the EC2 would be such that the very structure of the elements would begin to alter.

The crux of the matter was that the elements would get up to temperature by taking at night as much as they could and then they would come down during the

day. It would pass through a barrier where the metal changed its formation. It depended on how the Aga was run; some people didn't get it up to that point. My own electric Aga was one of the very first ones and I haven't really had a problem at all.

We looked after people having problems and we looked long and hard to find elements that were up to the job. We also, once we had determined the point of the heat barrier, changed things so they would never reach that point. The heat build up would stop short of that point.

Later in 1985, the EC2 was modified, with three banks of elements fitted as a further measure designed to avoid problems. 'And it has gone on to be a very popular model. Those Agas are still out there and people are delighted with them. I think the electric Aga now is as good as any. It's a damn

VIP visitor:
Prime Minister
Margaret
Thatcher
with Aga's
Arthur Price

Welcome to Emmerdale

In its 1989 souvenir supplement in the *Shropshire Star*, Glynwed announced that its jewel-in-the-crown products were about to become stars in a popular TV soap. 'The Aga and the Rayburn cookers often appear in television programmes,' the piece read. 'In fact, the Aga was the subject of one of BBC2's *Classic Design* [sic] series, joining such cult objects as Levi jeans, Volkswagen Beetle and the London Underground map. Soon, the Aga and the Rayburn will be 'starring together' in *Emmerdale Farm*, with a Rayburn Nouvelle installed in Home Farm and Annie having a brand new Aga cooker in the farm kitchen.'

good cooker,' Alan Bishop added, pointing out that the very nature of the Aga involved inherent testing challenges.

The problem with the Aga and all its developments is how do you accelerate the testing of the working cycle of something that is on all the while? With the lids, we have a thing that lifts the lids up and down day after day after day. With a car, you could run the engine to simulate a year's driving, but you can't do anything like that with the Aga because it is on all the while. With the Aga, running it constantly is not an artificial test; it's how it works.

Saluting an Aga stalwart

Alan Bishop (pictured left) is one of the great Aga institutions. He joined Allied Ironfounders in 1960 as an office boy and rose through the ranks to become Managing Director 29 years later. 'It was my first job,' he says, looking back on a lifetime with the Aga. 'I was 16 and straight from school. Basically I filled in and did almost everything. But it did mean I got to know all the departments and what was going on. Castings, purchasing, stock control, everything. I was on less than £1 a week when I started. I was the lowest paid on the site. I didn't really dream of one day becoming the managing director. It just came. There were quite a few of us around at that time and every year they took on a new office boy and so we moved up into other jobs.'

A year later, he was moved into the costing office and, in 1965, was promoted to Assistant Cost Accountant. 'That was another good grounding because I got to know the whole factory.' From there, he rose to become Cost Accountant and then, in the 1980s, Financial Accountant and, later, Financial Controller under the Group Finance Director.

Alan Bishop was made a director in 1983 and finally MD in 1989 when his close friend and mentor Arthur Price retired. When Alan in turn retires, he will have clocked up more than 42 years' service to the Aga, 23 of them as a director.

It was a 29-year career ladder from office boy to Managing Director! We worked hard and we worked long hours, but the thing is I never applied for any of my promotions. I was invited to an interview once – for Finance Director – but they came back after an hour and I was told I had the job.

It was the same with MD and I think it reflects well on the company. They always used to say, 'Look, when you're ready, we'll put those stripes on your shoulder.' And they were right.

I really got to know every aspect of the company and the Aga. At one time if you had asked me about any casting of the Aga I could have given you the serial number, the pattern number, what weight it was.

It's all those sort of things that matter. And Arthur was here all those years and I worked with him as I rose through the ranks.

It was not all plain sailing, however. Towards the end of 1989, just a short while after taking over the reins of the Aga division, the new Managing Director became embroiled in an industrial dispute at the Ketley site.

We did go through some rough times. We had a major five-week strike. It was all to do with the 37-hour week. We were on 39 hours and the unions were insisting [on 37]. Normally, we'd never had a strike, but if the unions could get into Glynwed, into one factory, with a 37-hour working week then they could go through it [the industry]. It was very difficult. My wife had relations in the works, but I never really had a problem with it. National union officials became involved and the *Shropshire Star* was loving it, but it never became nasty.

And it was the only time we'd had any real problems. In the factory, I always say that people don't leave unless we fire them – and we very rarely fire them. It's still a job for life here and that's rare. Last time I looked, the average length of service here – including the shops and Coalbrookdale – was eleven years plus. Considering that we took on shops only in the last five years, it's an impressive record.

The strike – which never materially affected sales of the Aga because distributors would usually hold six or seven weeks' worth of stock – was resolved when Glynwed pledged to introduce the shorter working week once the practice became more established within the ironfounding industry

within which it was a major player. The promise was honoured over the next two years.

Neither the first major strike in the Aga's history nor the initial problems associated with early EC2 models could, however, dent the reputation of the world's best-known range cooker. Overseas sales in key markets, such as Eire and the Netherlands, were accelerating and, in the UK, Glynwed benefited from a decade of decidedly conspicuous consumption.

Fuelled by a memorable housing boom, the dawn of the age of the microchip and the advent of Yuppie culture, these were the years when Barbour wax jackets were considered *de rigueur* in the city, the trend for nouvelle cuisine dominated a resurgence in interest in eating out, and style guides cited the Aga as the essential appliance in any Chelsea kitchen with good form.

And, as the decade drew to a close, record sales figures were seeing 8,000 new owners a year joining the Aga family.

Glynwed celebrated its fiftieth birthday in the final year of the decade and 60 years in the UK of its prize product, the Aga. In a souvenir supplement in the *Shropshire Star*, under the headline 'A celebration of quality and style over 60 years', Glynwed paid tribute to the Aga and the people who make it. Inside the historic Coalbrookdale foundry, Philip Upton was pictured dressing a flue pipe; Sean Harris was seen loading Aga fronts for shotblasting; and Eurwen Davies and Rona Tyrer (pictured left) were seen during the core-making process.

'1989 is an important year,' said Alan Bishop, who was pictured at his desk. He went on to explain the significance of exports to markets including Eire, Belgium, France, the Netherlands, Switzerland, Canada, United States of America, New Zealand, and even the Falkland Islands. 'Occasional orders for appliances and spares,' said the article, 'are received from Tanzania, Kenya and Japan. America is an important market for the Aga,' continued Alan Bishop, 'especially for the four-oven model.

'We are developing our strategy of further involvement in the European market and the Aga is undergoing stringent examination at test houses in Germany and Sweden (its original birthplace!) We expect to obtain the necessary approvals and start selling into these countries before long.'

And so it became…

The brand's advertising
during the eighties – such
as this example for the
electric Aga – provides an
entertaining snapshot of
the fashions and attitudes
of the time

1990-1999

Are you living
comfortably?

As the worst excesses of the 1980s were discarded – tossed aside like the unwanted *lollo rosso* leaves at the heart of a nouvelle cuisine offering – so Britain rebelled against the idea of self and retreated into a period of retrospection and a return to 'family values' and lifestyles built around personal comfort rather than the vacant style of the black ash-and-chrome era.

The decade that saw Margaret Thatcher step down as Conservative Party leader, the arrival of the UK's first television home-shopping channel, the launch of the National Lottery and the introduction of supermarket Sunday opening, was – in a way not dissimilar to Wilsonian Britain in the 1960s – shaped again by technology.

Nowhere was this more evident than in the home; this was the age of 'thinking machines' – computer-driven washing machines and dishwashers that used microchips to gauge the size of a load and alter the amount of water needed accordingly; halogen lamps which cooked 'by light'; and vacuum cleaners with built-in filters to alleviate problems for asthma sufferers.

In her Good Housekeeping book *Every Home Should Have One*, Jan Boxshall perceptively charts how this increasing reliance on technology was accompanied by a move toward more revisionist ideals.

Although there is now a huge reliance on high-tech gadgets, there has also been a reaction away from the 'designer' style of the 1980s, with a trend towards a more natural and, ironically, old-fashioned look. Natural wood, or wood-look laminates, quarry-tiled floors and rustic pine tables are the most popular kitchen style, and in contrast to the 1950s and 1960s kitchen, in which appliances were proudly displayed as badges of status, the modern preference is to hide them away in cupboards.

There has been a backlash against the 'fully fitted' kitchen, with a return to free-standing cupboards, dressers and cookers. Classic kitchen appliances are now competing against the plastics monopoly…and the Aga,

Aga advertising in the nineties majored on comfortable living and, unusually for the brand, regularly featured men

the epitome of country-kitchen style which itself has weathered almost 70 years of domestic change, is selling well (boosted by the free advertising given by the 'Aga sagas').

Indeed contemporary Aga advertising aimed to maximise the cooker's appeal amongst those looking for a return to traditional values. 'Though fashions in kitchen styling may come and go,' read one brochure entitled *Aga: It's a way of life*, 'the Aga design is timeless. An evergreen that complements every style of kitchen, from traditional farmhouse to ultra-modern kitchens of today... Small wonder, then, that an Aga becomes a friend for life.'

The first signs that the Aga was alive to the changing tastes in the 1990s British home came in 1991, when Glynwed introduced a new colour – jade – to the Aga range.

Then, the following year, came two more – claret and emerald – while brown, never a particularly popular hue and today

a relative rarity, was withdrawn.

The emphasis on colour remained throughout the decade. In September 1996, British Racing Green and pewter were introduced (as the dark green option was re-named Hunter Green) and red and emerald were withdrawn. Golden yellow and royal blue were unveiled in August of 1997, meaning the Aga palette now comprised a total of 13 colours: eight in the standard range and five in the select range, although one of these, the red, was deleted from the latter a year later.

Testimonials from Aga owners used in advertising of the day reveal the trend toward a homelier feel to the kitchen and the importance of colour choice.

'I was brought up with an Aga and we chose a pewter four-oven plus module as it seemed to fit our sixteenth-century kitchen,' said Sarah More-Molyneux, of Loseley Park near Guildford. 'It's always warm, always friendly and we love it!'

'I can't imagine life without one and Edward and Harriet, my children, also love the Aga,' said Belinda Marshall of Pattingham near Wolverhampton. 'The whole appeal of the Aga is to do with lifestyle and I chose Hunter Green because it's nature's colour.'

And Phil and Wendy Baskerville, of Eccleshall in Staffordshire, added: 'As it's a north-facing kitchen, it needed to be a warm colour and we chose claret because it blends in with our bricks and fitted the kitchen perfectly.'

Aga owner seeks Companion

But it was five years later that Glynwed launched the most radical – and, to some die-hard devotees, the most contentious – new Aga product so far. The Module, unveiled in January 1996, was, and remains, a conventional electric cooker clothed in traditional Aga styling and intended to fit on to the left-hand side of the range.

It was joined in October of the same year by the Companion, a freestanding version.

Initially, both were available only with electric hobs and fan-assisted oven; in 1998, however, Aga launched models with gas hobs. Finally, the company also offered customers the option of replacing the warming plate on new four-oven Agas with an electric ceramic hob 'providing you with even more cooking options'.

The launch of the new, conventional appliances was a brave move. On the one hand, dyed-in-the-wool Aga owners could not see the logic of a company which had traded for so many years on the virtues of stored-heat Aga cooking launching a conventional hob ostensibly designed to 'complement' the Aga, but which, they feared, might actually undermine those claimed attributes. If the Aga cooks better and does everything, they would argue, why are the Companion and Module needed?

On the other hand, marketing executives with Glynwed saw two potential consumer groups going untapped by the traditional approach. First, were those who felt in some way not quite ready to make the leap to cooking the Aga way without the reassurance of a medium with which they were familiar and comfortable. They wished to buy into the Aga lifestyle, but needed to know they had a fallback position.

The second group – perhaps a little ironically – was existing Aga owners. A significant number, research revealed, occasionally opted to cook on the electric or gas cooker that had remained in their kitchens after the Aga was installed.

The marketing logic here was clear: these customers might just as well be using an Aga-branded appliance perfectly in keeping with their Aga range.

Simon Page, who became Marketing Director of Aga-Rayburn after the launch of the Module and Companion, believes that not only was the decision the right one, but also that the gamble has paid off. He believes the decade to be among the most significant in the Aga's 80-year life.

'The Companion and Module increase the flexibility of what an Aga does and it's about overcoming some of the misconceptions about the Aga. It is sometimes easier to give people a solution to the misconceptions they may have than to try to disabuse them of that view.'

'The timeless qualities of the Aga have been consistent and have led to an image which is quintessentially British and stands for a quintessentially British way of life...' Simon Page

'I think all the timeless qualities of the Aga have been consistent – everything that allows Aga its special position – [and] have led to an image which is quintessentially British and stands for a quintessentially British way of life.'

He is convinced that the Module and Companion answer a specific need some customers have for choice.

It increases the flexibility of what an Aga does and it's about overcoming some of the misconceptions about the Aga. It is sometimes easier to give people a solution to the misconception they may have than to try to disabuse them of that view. There is no doubt that there is a significant minority – it may be more than that – of Aga owners who have another cooker that they use in conjunction with the Aga. They might as well have something that has the inherent values of an Aga.

'To the Aga what Pavarotti is to opera'

Mary Berry, author of the *The Aga Book* and widely regarded as the first lady of Aga cookery writers, has noticed how the Aga has reflected changing social patterns within the home. It has, she says, proven to be consummately flexible.

When one thinks how long I have been cooking on the Aga – though that's not as long as many who grew up with Agas in the family home – it's amazing how things have changed.

When I first started I did many more casseroles; long, slow, tender cooking. Then, we were very pleased to have slow-roasted meat, like a pot-roast of silverside with lovely vegetables.

Now people do not buy as many joints. That's simply not how we are cooking now. The times have changed. I remember when women who had Agas did

Cook and food writer Mary
Berry is regarded as the
'first lady' of Aga cookery
writers, sharing with the
brand a reputation for
enduring popularity

This Aga is hot...

In the summer of 1996, in the third issue of *Aga Magazine*, the quarterly title for members of the Aga community, appeared the following announcement:

'A two-oven oil-fired Aga was dismantled and stolen from a house in Swalcliffe, near Banbury in Oxfordshire, in March and readers are asked to check details if they are offered a second-hand Aga or parts.

'Details: works order no. M922510; cooker serial no. AO54377; colour dark green (code L 30-22 v -30-61 b+10-71)...'

Defining the meaning of the 'Aga saga'

From Jilly Cooper to Joanna Trollope, the Aga has featured in countless books colloquially known as 'Aga sagas'.

The term is officially defined as 'a popular novel set in middle-class surroundings of the type that typically own Aga cookers'.

Throughout the nineties, the Aga was portrayed as representing the very best of traditional living

not work. Now they go out to work, so they have much less time to cook. We are also so well travelled now that we want to cook, for example, dishes from all over the world and our meat and our fish is cooked for much shorter times than ever before.

Something that is not widely known is that I think Aga have re-calibrated the simmering oven. Before, people relied on the simmering plate because it truly simmered. And they would do porridge overnight in the simmering oven, for example. You can't really do that easily now because I believe the simmering oven temperature has been raised. That's excellent because it shows how the Aga is moving with the times.

I think with the Module and Companion that Aga have been very clever. The microwave is cold and white in the corner. But, going back to women having such a full life now, when one comes into the kitchen the Aga gives you a welcome; it is warm and it is ready. [Equally] it is not a bad thing to have a cooker on the side if you need a specific temperature. I have a Companion in the kitchen and recently had 30 people for Sunday lunch; even my four-oven Aga couldn't have done all that alone.

Having said that, when I first became cookery editor on *Ideal Home* magazine, I said to Aga that I needed to know the precise oven temperatures for the Aga. I wrote them down on a piece of card and put it in a drawer in the kitchen. I have never, ever used that card! With the Aga you do need to learn in the beginning; you have to listen at the start to fully understand the simplicity of the Aga. Those people who like to knock the Aga do so, I think, because

Roads across America

Between 1996 and 1999, two senior Aga employees were asked to make frequent trips from Glynwed's head offices in Birmingham to the United States as part of a sales drive to boost awareness of the Aga in America.

In October 1996 alone, David Coath and Dawn Roads visited six states, travelling more than 3,800 miles. Armed with training manuals and brochures, the pair also met seven key Aga dealers and 200-plus potential purchasers.

Dawn Roads, who joined Aga as a home economist in 1984, remembers how the Americans' reactions to the Aga revealed much about the cooker's international standing.

'They would say "Gee, where's the burner?" or "What do you do with this?". And it was interesting to find out how they knew about the Aga. For many, the first time they heard about the Aga was in English novels by Rosamund Pilcher, Dick Francis and Agatha Christie. Others had come across the Aga while visiting friends or family in the UK, or while stationed or working over here.'

Dawn and David, whose exploits stateside were featured in the BBC documentary *Aga and Their Owners*, struggled on occasions to get through US customs. 'We were

they are used to conventional cookers and have never actually taken the trouble to understand it.

Mary Berry lives with her husband in Penn in Buckinghamshire, where since 1990 more than 12,000 Aga owners have attended her Aga Workshops, held in her 'great barn of a kitchen'. She trained in catering at Bath College of Home Economics and at the Paris *Cordon Bleu*, but knew from an early age that she did not want to go into the restaurant business. Instead, she 'wanted to teach'. She began as cookery editor on *Housewife* magazine before moving to *Ideal Home*.

She became well known, long before the explosion of celebrity TV chefs and the national obsession with cooking fashions. She presented networked cookery programmes for Thames Television, appeared on Radio 4's *Woman's Hour*, did monthly guest slots on Debbie Thrower's Radio 2 programme, and starred in BBC1's *Mary Berry's Ultimate Cakes* and

Mary Berry at Home.

The *Mail on Sunday*'s YOU magazine famously said of her: 'Mary Berry is to Aga what Pavarotti is to opera.'

It was the arrival of *The Aga Book* (published by Aga-Rayburn) however, that established her as the pre-eminent Aga writer of her day. *Mary Berry's New Aga Cookbook* (Hodder Headline, 1999) followed and September 2002 was due to see publication of a third book, *Cook Now, Eat Later*. Though Aga cooking guidelines will be given, this is not planned to be an Aga volume.

In 1998, Mary Berry was featured alongside other Aga devotees in a BBC2 documentary, *Agas and Their Owners*. While undoubtedly entertaining television, the programme has been criticised for portraying many of the participants as, at best, utterly obsessed with their cookers and, at worst, decidedly odd.

The documentary spotlighted an array of colourful Aga owners. We saw General Sir Richard and Lady Inga Lawson and the collection of stopped at Atlanta airport once. It was a Sunday I remember and we were travelling from Atlanta to Minnesota, I think. We were picked out after the X-ray imaging camera revealed the kitchen knives in our bags!'

Though awareness of the Aga in the US was limited, Dawn Roads was impressed by the passion for the cooker shown by those Americans who did know of it.

'One couple in New London had purchased a brand new stainless steel range cooker. When they saw the Aga, they said they weren't even going to open the packaging. Others brought home-baked bread and cakes to our demonstrations and others would travel two hours to come to see us or stay overnight, such was the level of interest.'

parrots they kept in the kitchen with the Aga. There was the police officer and his wife who had an Aga installed in the village police house; an elderly couple still getting sterling service out of their vintage, solid-fuel Aga; the housewife who organised classical music concerts in her kitchen, with attendees arranged in chairs around the Aga; and the elderly Aga owner proudly showing off her invention of an 'Aga hairdryer'.

The programme, which was promoted as exploring 'the passionate world of the British middle class and this most eccentric of cookers', also featured contributions from Jocasta Innes, Richard Maggs, now a regional sales manager for Aga-Rayburn, and the inventor and entrepreneur James Dyson.

Two so-called 'Aga haters' were fielded: food columnist Digby Anderson and the design historian Stephen Calloway. The former criticised those who 'worship the Aga, rather than use it', while the latter was yet more damning. 'I think,' he said to camera, 'there is

a conspiracy among Aga owners that they belong to this club. You are invited to partake of the rituals and approach the holiest of holies.

'And, if you have the temerity to say that you don't like Agas, it is as if you have said something blasphemous. It has become one of the great blasphemies of modern life.'

Mary Berry – who, despite being an authoritative Aga voice was, significantly, on screen for considerably less time than most of those interviewed – remains unimpressed by the documentary's voyeuristic feel.

Surely, the Aga is about cooking? They spent the entire day here, but they were really only trying to find difficult people, odd people. It was absolutely stupid. They said they were doing something journalistic, but there was this sense that they were laughing at us, poking fun at us. Where were the typical Aga owners? There was not one farmer's wife, who uses

My love affair with the Aga

In the introduction to her original cookbook, which by 1999 was in its eighth reprint, Mary Berry writes of her love affair with the Aga…

'Until I owned an Aga I never fully understood how Aga owners could be so ecstatic about a cooker. Now I totally understand and am devoted to mine.

'When asked to explain my feelings about the Aga, a variety of thoughts flash through my mind. I see myself coming downstairs on a cold February morning, walking straight to the warm heart of the kitchen, the Aga. Leaning against it as I get my thoughts straight for the day, meanwhile moving the pile of sheets that have been airing all night on top of the simmering plate's insulated cover.

'Then I see one of the boys coming in after getting soaked on the golf course. No problem, the damp clothes go up to dry in the warm air above the Aga. I can also see the happy face of someone snuggling into an Aga-warmed jacket before going out!

'I can recall the mallard duck that hatched out in the cupboard next to the Aga, what excitement that was! I can see Bumble, our much-loved black retriever, and indeed his son too, stretched out beside the Aga and being too old to move over because I wanted to cook! It is said

the Aga and really knows the Aga? They did not give us the typical Aga owner; they were only interested in the most eccentric, the oddest.

Producer and director of *Agas and Their Owners* for BBC Bristol was Jane Treays, now making programmes for Granada and Channel 4. She is unrepentant:

Of course we set out to find the most eccentric. You know I couldn't have simply made something worthy and adoring; it was a film about people's perceptions of the Aga.

I have an Aga – have had for many years – and I love it; I wouldn't be without it. But God it would have been boring if we had done what some people would have wanted the programme to have been.

Treays makes the point that the programme was a 'celebration of

the Aga and how people see it' and that Aga provided contact details for many of the participants.

'I didn't set out to find people who put girl guides' uniforms on bits of bamboo to make a hairdryer! Four million people watched and we had such a great time making it. I am not remotely bothered by any criticism; goodness me it did them [Aga] an awful lot of good.'

In the same year, it was a major reorganisation of the Aga business itself that made headlines, this time within Britain's financial press. Glynwed International plc declared its intention to focus on just two core growth activities: its pipe systems business and, importantly, consumer and foodservice products. It was this second grouping which was to become, three years later in March 2001, the current Aga Foodservice Group, opening yet another chapter in the story of the kitchen classic…

of the House of Commons that it's like joining the best club in the country. I think owning an Aga is a bit similar; certainly, when you meet another Aga owner it is like discovering an instant friend.'

Aga authors' recipes for publishing success

It is estimated that in excess of 8,000 individual cookery books are in print in the UK. Of these only a handful have been devoted to Aga cooking.

Mary Berry is just one of a small army of food writers whose output has centred on the Aga and its special attractions. She has produced two celebrated Aga cookbooks: *The Aga Book* (Glynwed, 1990) and *Marry Berry's New Aga Cookbook* (Hodder Headline, 1999).

Louise Walker is among the most prolific in her field, having produced four titles so far – the *Four Seasons Aga Cookery Book, The Traditional Aga Book of Slow Cooking, The Traditional Aga Cookery Book* and *The Traditional Aga Party Book* (all by Absolute Press) – with more planned.

In 1998, Rosemary Moon wrote her *Aga Cookbook* (David & Charles/Aga-Rayburn) and in October 2002, Ebury Press published Amy Willcock's *Aga Cooking*.

Right and below:
A full range of accessories and regular Aga demonstrations added to the Aga lifestyle

Beyond 2000

Back to the future

If the 1990s for the Aga were about consolidation of the brand as it moved through its eighth decade, the dawn of the new millennium saw a restructuring of the business behind the famous marque and a sea-change in how the cooker was marketed.

In the first year of the new decade, the Aga's parent company, Glynwed, announced that it intended to split into two quite distinct businesses: one centred on its traditional pipe systems operations and the other on its consumer and foodservice division, fast developing in the City a reputation for performance.

Less than a year later, in January 2001, that plan became a reality when Glynwed sold the pipe systems division to the Belgian Group Etex for £786 million. Two months later, the Aga's owner was officially given a new name: the Aga Foodservice Group.

The move – applauded by shareholders and the City alike – marked the advent of a period of unprecedented acquisition. First, however, the Aga Foodservice Group (AFG) had plans to take its best-known product into uncharted territory with the launch of Agalinks.com, a major internet portal site. The Aga – at the ripe old age of 79 – was about to debut in a starring role on the world wide web.

The Aga enters the internet age…

Six months in planning and development, Agalinks.com represented a £3 million investment on the part of the Aga's owners. It was unveiled on 2nd February 2001. In a promotional leaflet to accompany the launch, Aga described its objectives for the site:

> Agalinks.com has one very simple aim – to bring you the very best of the internet. There's a vast array of information out there and sometimes it can be difficult to find exactly what you're looking for. Trawling the internet can be both frustrating and time-consuming.
>
> Aga recognise this and we have designed our site with this in mind. We've brought together experts in various fields to give you

Agalinks – the internet resource launched by Aga in 2001 – promised the 'very best of life on the net'

concise, practical and ultimately useful information on subjects that affect us all. From passports to pets, from antiques to apples, Agalinks has it covered.

On launch, the site consisted of 12 'channels' – Cooking & The Kitchen, Life & Travel, Pets, House & Home, Art & Antiques, Walking & Cycling, Financial Services, Wealth Management, The Garden, Heritage, Health & Wellbeing and Country Living – designed to appeal to both Aga owners and non-owners alike.

'If you're stuck for dinner-party ideas,' trumpeted the advertising literature, 'confused about ISAs, fancy getting away to Tuscany, or wish you could remember the Latin name for the primrose, then Agalinks will have the answer.'

'Agalinks.com is such an excellent idea,' said Mary Berry. 'With more and more people looking to the web for ideas, a dedicated Aga portal will be a great place to find inspiration.'

Novelist Jilly Cooper added: 'Agas are gorgeous things and if Agalinks allows one to learn more about their gorgeousness then it will be a wonderful thing.'

Richard Scarre, Operations Director at Agalinks, steered the project from informal discussion of an idea through to launch amid a flourish of media coverage and a six-figure advertising spend.

'The launch date is etched on my mind, of course it is. Anything like that has its trials and tribulations. When you try to pull a number of strands together – both content and technical – it becomes a complex undertaking. It was launched with a lot of hard work from a lot of people from several different organisations.'

The idea first formed during several late-night brainstorming sessions in the autumn of 1999 at Aga's head office at Headland House in Birmingham. The discussions involved Richard Scarre and William McGrath, Chief Executive of AFG. 'He and I,' says the former, 'were throwing ideas around on what we could do to

Aga online: Richard Scarre, Operations Director of Agalinks, and Laura James, Editor of the site

capitalise on the brand presence we have and the internet. We were stress-testing the concept.'

From March until July 2000, a project team worked with external consultants KPMG on assessing aspects of the proposition, including market analysis and selected focus groups, before work began on design and construction of the site itself.

Richard Scarre: 'We came to the conclusion that the potential audience was quite large and, because the Aga is an aspirational product, there was actually a huge number of people who were aspiring to the Aga way of life without actually living it yet. The constituency for Agalinks widened out to include all of those people.'

In the summer of 2000 the proposition was presented to the Glynwed board. 'Their view,' says Richard Scarre, 'was that it was worth doing, but the Aga brand represented the crown jewels and we should take care not to drop it!'

Glynwed allocated £3 million to the three-year Agalinks business plan, the bulk of the spend substantially weighted into the first twelve months. A number of agencies were then recruited to take the idea from spreadsheet to live internet site.

The portal was designed by a team from Precedent. It was 'hosted' on the internet by Globix, built by Smart 421 with editorial content supplied by e-Space and contract publishing agency Summerhouse.

'The hardest part of that really was the technical infrastructure – to design and build and launch on time,' says Richard Scarre. 'And it was just one day later than had been approved. There was blood, sweat and tears, but we got through it.'

By the time of the site's first birthday, Agalinks had built up a formidable following within the Aga community. More than 75,000 people had signed up as registered users and each month the site clocked up some 80,000 visitor sessions.

'We are continually looking to develop the site,' says Richard Scarre, 'in concert with what we're doing with Aga as a brand and the

The management team at Aga were determined to expose the Aga to a new kind of customer and, in September 2001, a radically different advertising strategy – the Iron Age campaign – was devised to take the world's most famous cooker to a younger, more urban audience

product developments that are coming from Aga, as well as what the group is doing in establishing itself as the premium home-fashion business.'

Editor of Agalinks is consumer journalist Laura James. She believes a key ingredient in the success of the site is the breadth of content offered.

> When I was asked to be Editor of the site, I have to admit I was slightly nervous at the prospect. Aga owners have a real relationship with their cookers and to succeed Agalinks would have to bring to life all of the values associated with Aga.
> The site has wide appeal and is used by both Aga owners and non-owners alike. We have an intelligent, free-thinking audience, so it's important for us to provide information and entertainment that is topical, relevant and really useful.
> Obviously, the Cooking

& The Kitchen channel is a huge success. But more tangential subjects have huge appeal, too. The Pets channel in particular benefits from a great deal of audience participation and we are very lucky to receive huge support from top chefs, celebrities and experts in all sorts of areas, as well, of course, as the wider Aga community itself.
> And Agalinks is great to work on – every day is different and the breadth of subject matter we deal with is truly amazing. From Marmite to marmosets, it's all there!

As Agalinks found its feet in the digital world, the newly liberated and cash-rich Aga Foodservice Group set its sights on growth. The new group made its first significant strategic move in July 2001, when it expanded its retail operations through the acquisition of Fired Earth, one of the UK's leading interior finishes companies

Aga and weird wide web
While the Aga Foodservice Group has Agalinks.com, the Aga-owning community across the world has inhabited the internet with its own rash of dedicated websites, some of them charming, some decidedly odd…

Succour for the have-nots…
At www.agawannabe.com our American hosts have – presumably with tongue firmly planted in cheek – created an internet site dedicated to those who aspire to own an Aga, but alas do not.

'A wannabe,' the introduction tells us, 'is someone who enjoys the look and style of the Aga, someone who covets the cooking experience of the Aga, but does not, sadly, own one.'

Help is at hand, however. 'There are plenty of things a wannabe can do to while [sic] away his time while looking hopefully forward to some far future day when his Aga-less state will come to an end, but the fact remains that even all of those activities fall short of the reality of actually owning an Aga.

'If you're not, or have never been, a wannabe, you'll never fully understand the longing. If you currently are a wannabe, you don't care about anybody else's longing because you're too busy wanting an Aga yourself.

'If you're an Aga owner, shame on

perhaps best known for its tiles and related flooring products. The business logic behind the acquisition was clear: with both the Aga and its new sister company renowned worldwide for craftsmanship, traditional values and an innovative approach to home styling, the synergies between the two companies would lead to the opportunity to share respective customer bases and retail outlets.

In November came the first outward sign of these synergies when the Fired Earth Inspirations store attached to the company's head office in Adderbury in Oxfordshire was re-worked to include an Aga Studio showcasing products from both companies and featuring a cookery demonstration area. Less than five months later a second Aga Studio had been unveiled at a new Fired Earth concept store at Warmington Mill near Peterborough. More such stores are planned.

The acquisition brought other benefits. Artists with AFG and Fired Earth worked together to develop a style palette for interior

design and, according to an Aga spokesman, 'there are plans to develop paints and tiles to match the Aga range'. Furthermore, the Aga – once considered by some potential purchasers to be difficult to locate – was, almost overnight, highly visible in 55 Fired Earth outlets across the UK.

…and then the Iron Age
In tandem with an ambitious acquisitions policy, the management team at AFG was determined to expose the Aga to a new kind of customer. In September 2001 a radically different advertising strategy was devised to take the world's most famous cooker to a younger, more urban audience. It was called the Iron Age campaign. Publicity material supplied to consumer journalists explained why:

> Aga is an extremely
> strong brand with
> an outstanding sales record.
> Its name has entered the
> English language as a
> generic term for range

you if you haven't invited one of your Aga-less brethren to share for a few hours in the bounty of your fortune! You, above all others, know the depth of the longing.'

Notwithstanding such doom and gloom, our hosts do go on to suggest some 'things to do while you're waiting'… 'OK, so you're a wannabe….what are you going to do until the day finally arrives when you resolve all the obstacles between you and your Aga destiny?

'Well, here are a few ideas: Play "How would I cook this in an Aga?" every time you prepare a meal; try to cook almost everything in your oven; browse the web looking for new sources of Aga information; hang around the major bookstore chains waiting for the latest British home magazines; buy an Aga cookbook from the same bookstore; find pictures of Aga cookers, scan them, and email them to me (I'll post them to the site); take daily temperature measurements of your kitchen, then add 2 degrees; go over what the floor plan will look like when the Aga arrives…again; thumb through the brochure you got at the product demonstration….again; join an email group and commiserate with other wannabes; wisely invest your money.'

cooker and it even has its own classification of literature – Aga sagas. Cliché or not, anything that can get a brand its own BBC2 documentary programme at prime-time on Christmas Eve and then be shown across the world has to be a gift.

Aga has now taken the bold step of challenging the pre-conceived ideas of who owns its cookers and is, for the first time in its history, broadening the appeal of its products to capture younger, more urban dwellers.

Entitled Iron Age, the campaign has two major elements. The first, based on Iron Age Man and Iron Age Woman, asks people to reconsider their preconceptions of Aga cookers. The second, based on the theme 'A sense of place, a sense of purpose', positions Aga as a design icon which

looks equally stunning in a contemporary as well as a traditional setting.

The £3m Iron Age campaign was distinguished as much by where advertisements were placed as by what they said. For the first time, consumers saw Aga adverts not only in *Country Living, Country Life, The Field* and *Good Housekeeping*, but in more fashion-conscious magazines such as the new-wave style-bible *Wallpaper*, and women's lifestyle magazines such as *Red, Marie Claire* and *Vogue*.

Simon Page, Marketing Director at AFG, believes the first years of the new millennium to be among the most exciting in the Aga's 80-year life and he is convinced Iron Age will deliver a broadened market while retaining the loyalty of the cooker's heartland customer base.

I think all the timeless qualities of the Aga have been consistent – everything that allows the Aga its

The key to the success of the Iron Age initiative will be the ability to speak to a new audience while retaining an awareness of the Aga's roots.

special position – have led to an image which is quintessentially British. If you think of Aga you do think of rolling fields, country kitchens, Sunday roast and rain at Wimbledon. That's what probably makes Aga so enduring as a brand and as a product. You have bought this romantic image as part of the *emotion* of owning an Aga, but actually when you get the Aga home, it does make a very different place in which to live.

Agas are warm; they are comfortable, they are solid and chunky. They are the sort of things that in the hurly-burly of life today – you get up at 7.00 in the morning, you get in at 7.30

at night, you have a hassled and stressful day – offer reassurance. You get back to this thing that is practical, simple to use, comfortable and warm and always there and, though talking of getting back to the mother's womb is a little strong as a statement, it is that sort of feeling. It's an oasis of certainty in the very difficult environment in which people live today. That is genuinely part of the reassurance that is the Aga.

I only became an Aga owner in the last 12 months. Up until then we were a household which lived in the lounge. We'd sit in the lounge and we'd talk and people would go off to do their own thing. Cooking

Right, it's time to get an Aga!

'I'm very excited. We've finally got a nice family house now. The only real reason we bought the house was because it felt nice, you know – a lot of light and it felt like a happy house.

'And when I came into the kitchen, I thought "right, time for an Aga I think". Jools had wanted one since we got married and when we got this place I didn't think stainless steel things would look quite right.

'Plus, I don't believe that there's anything you can't cook on an Aga. The way that I cook, these days is if I'm going to have breakfast, even just a fried egg on toast, I've got about four minutes to do it. So I do need that immediate heat. If I have to wait for a grill to pre-heat - even if it's just five minutes - then it's impossible: I'm late.

'So it's a lifestyle thing as well. I love doing scallops straight on to the simmering plate on the Aga, as well as medallions of beef and lamb chops. I even put the lid down sometimes if what I'm cooking is not too thick. It self cleans as well. I just put down the lid and when I come down in the morning it's

was my wife Patty's province; nobody else cooked, although we had a very nice Rangemaster cooker. Since owning the Aga, we now live in the kitchen. If people come to see us, we don't go into the dining room or the lounge, we stay in the kitchen.

I now cook more than I have ever cooked since I was a student and our children, Robert and Emily, who are 10 and 13, are quite happy cooking cakes and all sorts of things on the Aga. It has become a genuine focus of family life. That's an enduring quality of the Aga: it becomes a focus of family relationships.

The key to the success of the Iron Age initiative, Simon Page believes, will be the ability to speak to a new audience while retaining an awareness of the Aga's roots. 'What we definitely don't want to do with the Iron Age campaign is to lose all those core values that the

Aga stands for. If you lost those, you would lose everything that the Aga is about. But in a sense, the Aga's strength is also its weakness. Agas have actually always been more urban, more metropolitan than perhaps the image would belie.'

He likens the re-alignment of marketing emphasis to changes that have taken place with another great British brand.

At one point Land Rover made the big Defender, that really was the country workhorse: it did the job on the farm; you put the sheep in the back; and it developed something of a cult following in rural life. Then somebody at Land Rover was sitting there and said: 'Well, where do we go next? How do we grow Land Rover without damaging what we have got at the moment?' Out of that were spawned the Range Rover, the Discovery and the Freelander. But if I said:

gone! Jules hadn't cooked for a long, long time, but she's got really good at stews and stuff. We've been doing things on my mum's Aga. Whacking the thing on the top, browning off some meat, chucking a load of stuff in, and whacking it in the simmering oven and coming back eight hours later and it's wicked.

'I think it [an Aga] makes people better cooks. It's like that vegetarian thing. Serious vegetarians who love food, are generally really good cooks because they have to duck and dive a little bit to get around the fact that they're not eating meat. It's like that with people who have an Aga; they're generally technically better cooks because they understand cooking.

'There are so many aspects of cooking that I think are overlooked, I mean actual technical cooking. Why are you trying to wok-fry something? Why are you trying to braise or stew something? I mean really, you can buy an average bit of old meat and if you cook it right it's going to be good. If you have a fantastic bit of meat and inspiration with herbs and you cook it right, then it's going to be genius isn't it?'

JAMIE OLIVER, (PICTURED OPPOSITE)
LONDON

'Tell me about Land Rover today', you would still talk about an image of mud-spattered mudguards and four-wheel drive.

Land Rover now has more than one audience buying into this rugged four-wheel-drive concept. And they know that if they can understand the needs of each audience, they can modify the offering.

In an Aga we do that already. If you live in the country, we can give you an oil Aga, a gas Aga, we can give you an electric Aga. Then, sitting within the theme of the basic Aga product, you can have the Aga Classic, which looks like an Aga looked in the 1950s, you can have the contemporary styling of the timeless Aga – which is the one we sell the most of – you can have the Aga 2000, which has chrome fronts, or you can have the Aga Signature Collection, with more of

a design feel in the way it uses colour.

All of those things say that we are trying to meet the different needs of different customers within the context of the basic Aga.

The failing of Aga – even if we were not to try to move it forward but simply to stand still – would be to say that there is a stereotypical Aga owner. There is not. People who buy into the Aga way of life and become members of the Aga community are many and varied and we have to recognise that.

A good example of that sales philosophy, says Simon Page, is the Six-Four Series, a conventional cooker with Aga styling launched early in 2002. The model offers Aga good looks through an enamelled cast-iron exterior, coupled with electric ovens, grill and a six-burner gas hob. Following on from the Masterchef – the first modern conventional cooker from Aga, but

one which did not boast traditional styling – the Six-Four (pictured opposite), he says, is a particularly handsome creation.

'Really what we are saying is already we have a variety of Agas you can buy. The Six-Four Series means you can buy into a solid, cast-iron, hand-made, British-made product with all of the brand values of Aga, but which is not about saying we have a religious zeal about converting you to cooking in a particular way. We think the way the Aga original cooks is an absolutely beautiful way of cooking which produces marvellous food, but not everybody wants – or is able – to make that 'Road to Damascus' conversion.'

Simon Page, who speaks of the Aga with tangible affection, refers to the brand as the 'paternal head' of the varied products manufactured by the Aga Foodservice Group. He believes the key to the brand's future success to be logical, careful diversification while retaining a firm grip on what it is that makes the Aga special.

'What the group is saying is that it wants to be the custodian of a series of strong brands with strong customer goodwill and defendable positions within the marketplace. We are not saying we want to be the biggest in the world. What we are saying is that there will be people and markets around the world that want to buy high quality, well made household products.'

In April 2002, the group launched Omnia, a new Aga-manufactured range of contemporary cookware cast in iron but, significantly, designed to be used on any cooker. The range will sit alongside AFG's already established cookware collection.

And the summer saw the launch of two landmark new products – the first Aga refrigerator and Aga freezer, both boasting Aga styling and both manufactured by Williams Refrigeration, an Aga Foodservice Group company specialising in professional reach-in cabinets, freezers and cold rooms to the UK catering and restaurant trades. The advertising campaign surrounding these new products was planned to revolve around an Ice Age theme.

The new offerings will, say Aga, create a compelling portfolio of products for the discerning, style-conscious consumer.

Eyes on America

AFG has stated publicly that its aim is to become one of the world's leading home fashion retailers and in March 2002 it made an important step toward an increased international presence with the acquisition of Domain, an American home fashions business based in Boston and with 25 retail outlets along the eastern seaboard of the US.

While one in five of the 8,000-plus Agas sold each year goes abroad – the biggest overseas markets being Eire, Belgium and the Netherlands – just 400 Aga cookers a year are bought by Americans. Aga believes the US to be an important area of future growth.

2002 and beyond

Notwithstanding recent periods of great change, much about the Aga remains reassuringly constant. British consumers continue to prefer the traditional cream over any other colour (38% of all 2001 sales) with British Racing Green (16%) and dark blue (15%) following in the popularity stakes.

The two-oven, gas-fired Aga remains the most popular model, with almost one in three new Aga owners opting for this combination. Overall, the smaller models have retained their appeal, with two-oven models accounting for over half of all sales.

It would be wrong amid the flurry of high-profile acquisitions and the launch of so many Aga-associated products – to believe that development of the cooker *per se* has ceased.

Development is under way within the research and development facility at Ketley in the West Midlands on a five-oven Aga which promises even greater cooking flexibility and an all-new electric Aga which, for the first time, will not be based entirely on stored heat.

Simon Page believes such developments – coupled with the enduring appeal of the Aga way of life – will ensure a long life for the cooker invented in 1922.

You do have to say that invariably anyone looking forward at the kitchen of 2020 will be wrong. They always have been wrong, haven't they? But I see no reason why the Aga shouldn't feature in the kitchens of 2020.

The big thing is what is happening in life generally: we have fewer people doing more work, working longer hours. The pace of life is increasingly hectic and all the things designed to make life more simple are also all symbols of this changing pace of life and the lack of a firm foundation and what everyone wants at home –

sequel to *The Silence of the Lambs*. The lead, Hannibal Lecter, wants only the best. The director [Ridley Scott] specified Wuestof knives and Aga cookers! He'll be using a four-oven black in his home and we're doing a complete Aga shop with a two-oven cream Aga.'

In fact, things didn't quite work out to plan. An Aga was indeed in the final scene. Sadly, one could only see the Aga pipe.

For those keen to play the game of Aga-spotting, however, the cooker has featured in, among many others, the hit ITV drama *Cold Feet*, in the stage production of Agatha Christie's *The Mousetrap* and in the 1998 movie *Practical Magic*, starring Sandra Bullock and Nicole Kidman.

Despite myriad colours over the Aga's 80 years, cream remains the most popular

an anchor. What the Aga is one of those anchors.

Geoff Harrop, who joined Aga-Rayburn in 1997 and has been Managing Director of the company since 1999, believes the people behind the Aga brand have learned hard lessons in recent years.

He said: 'I think there was a stage when we lost sight of the philosophy that we needed to look after the customer. I am proud of how we have evolved as a company: we used to make things for people to buy; now we make things people want. We are doing now what the brand always promised.'

William McGrath is Chief Executive of the Aga Foodservice Group. He believes the Aga's heritage will also be its future. With footprints in history left around the world – from the Agas installed in the 1930s aboard the trains of Iraq Railways to the Aga that travelled with British scientists to the Antarctic – he is convinced the cooker will feature in kitchens for many years to come.

'In deciding to reorganise the business,' he says, 'we were searching for something that would take it forward. We had a great business, but one that needed to be given a little bit more freedom to develop. In the days of the old Glynwed there was sometimes resentment that the Aga accounted for 10 per cent of the business, but got 90 per cent of the attention. We decided that this was essentially the point.'

McGrath believes the focus should fall on three areas: retaining the respect and loyalty of the Aga's core market; redefining the socio-demographic appeal of the cooker in the UK to embrace a younger audience and ensuring the Aga is easily available to them; and the broadening of the Aga's appeal.

The Aga's heritage and reputation for solidity, performance and individuality will ensure continuing success in the UK. The Iron Age campaign will address the perceived need to reach new customers.

For both McGrath and Stephen Rennie, AFG's Group

'The Aga has such a strong presence in the lives of so many people that… I feel a flush of pride when I think about the 80 years it has been with us and the exciting times that still lie ahead'

Looking to the future: Aga Foodservice Group Chief Executive William McGrath

Operations Director, the acquisition of Domain in Boston is a fundamental plank of the last of those aims for the Aga, with New England specifically and the eastern seaboard of the US more generally providing the perfect platform for the campaign to sell America a taste of Britain.

'For the first time,' says William McGrath, 'the Aga in the United States will benefit from a dedicated American sales force. This is our first attempt to really crack the US. In the past, we have had heroics and plenty of good people [working in the US]. But now we need to take it from the point where film stars buy the Aga to the point where it is embraced as a mainstream American product.'

McGrath, an Oxford history graduate who first fell for the Aga while helping out with the potato picking on his sister's farm in the West Country, is in no doubt that the story of the Aga has many twists and turns yet to come.

'With the Aga there is a real continuum. Coalbrookdale from 1709; invention of the Aga in 1922. From Abraham Darby to the present day. So what we have set out to create is something that would build on this continuum, this sense of tradition, while having the courage not to live off the past.

'The Aga works today because it fits in so well. It is the little black dress of the interiors world. No one is ever indifferent about the Aga. It is intrinsically an interesting product.

'It also has such a strong presence in the lives of so many people that, yes, I do feel a flush of pride when I think about the 80 years it has been with us and the exciting times that still lie ahead…'

History in the making

Don Flack has lived and breathed the Aga since he was 15. Now retired, he started work at the Coalbrookdale foundry in Shropshire on 21st April 1952 and, when his friends and colleagues waved him off in March 2002, he had clocked up almost five decades of service to the plant where the Aga is cast. As he left the foundry for the last time, he turned round at the gates and said his own, very personal goodbye. 'I just stopped and said "Thank you, Coalbrookdale".'

Flack, who lives in Coleport, a few miles from the World Heritage Site at Coalbrookdale, started in the engineering pattern shop from school as an ancillary worker assembling parts.

'In those days,' he says, 'you were just lucky to have a job. The foundry was working a three-day week because there just wasn't the demand in what was then a very depressed economy. I started on eight shillings a day – £2 a week – but the management kindly said they couldn't pay for just three days, so I was paid for the full five.'

Today, the more mechanised foundry can, if required, turn out 60 Aga front panels a day. Back in the 1950s, according to Flack, the men at Coalbrookdale would manage between six and eight in Dante-esque conditions, surrounded by molten metal and searing heat, and assaulted by almost unbearable noise levels.

Back when I started, it was like the Black Hole of Calcutta. It was hell and it was dangerous work. I remember one chap joking to me that slavery was supposed to be going out, but at Coalbrookdale it was coming in! And another chap I remember was a Mr Chalkley. He was ex-military and over six feet tall. I was always having to look up at him. But when he finished there, I no longer had to do that – his back had arched that much.

It was exhausting work and, when you finished, you knew you had been working. These were the days when a horse and cart were still used to pull the castings.

Don Flack is keen to stress, however, that these

To visit the foundry is to take a step back in time, to an era when talented craftsmen who could work metallurgical magic with molten iron ruled the industrial world.

When Don Flack left Coalbrookdale for the last time, he had clocked up almost five decades at the foundry. Together with a group of colleagues, he built the famous gates

'I owe my life to Coalbrookdale. The camaraderie was similar to being in the army. We helped each other, we looked after each other. I was ready to retire and I wanted to retire, but I will miss it all very much. Fifty years is a big part of anyone's life.'

are 50-year-old memories and that not only have conditions improved immeasurably, but also that he cherishes his time at Coalbrookdale and Ketley, the sister plant he would visit at least once a week for meetings to discuss shortages of raw materials or modifications to the Aga castings.

Still, despite the conditions in the early days, it was a marvellous experience. I owe my life to Coalbrookdale. The camaraderie was similar to being in the army. We helped each other, we looked after each other. It is so very different now and health and safety at the foundry is the highest priority.

I was ready to retire and I wanted to retire, but I will miss it all very much. Fifty years is a big part of anyone's life.

When he turned 18, Flack was called up for his National Service and joined the King's Shropshire Light Infantry. His memories of this time prompt recollections of Coalbrookdale's own wartime service. There is an area of the foundry site known to those who work there as The Wing Shop; it is where, at the height of the Second World War, Fisher & Ludlow produced wings for the Lancaster. 'On the window ledges, you can still find the rivets used.'

Over 50 years, Flack advanced from ancillary worker to worker, charge hand, foreman and superintendent, before becoming one of the foundry managers in 1990. Throughout his time at the foundry he was never called to task by his superiors and – displaying a fortitude that would put many contemporary office workers to shame – managed an 18-year stint without a single day's absence due to illness. 'On my last day, though,' he says, 'I went in a little late.'

With more time on his hands, Flack now plans to indulge his love of engineering and hopes to bring to the market some of the domestic and automotive inventions he has been working on. 'I get a real kick

out of making things and I will look back on helping in a small way to make the Aga with great pride.'

Metallurgical magic

Even today, more than 80 years after its invention, that manufacturing process is one which the Aga's creator, Dr Gustaf Dalén, would not only recognise, but would also surely approve of.

There are more than 750,000 Agas installed in kitchens around the world. All have been hand built in the so-called Valley of Invention, birthplace of the Industrial Revolution. The casting is carried out at Coalbrookdale near Telford while the enamelling process that gives the Aga its famous and highly durable finish takes place at a second plant in nearby Ketley.

To visit the foundry is almost to take a step back in time, to an era when talented craftsmen who could work metallurgical magic with molten iron ruled the industrial world. Enormous furnaces burn and, with the molten iron manipulated at a staggering 1,500°C before being poured like treacle into moulds; it is an impressive spectacle.

Each Aga begins life as a detailed drawing. From this, carpenters produce a wooden master pattern. The next stage is to create a more robust aluminium template, which is then pressed into moulding sand leaving an impression for the molten iron to be poured into.

When the iron has cooled, it forms a solid casting. It is this casting that is sent to be shot-blasted, a process which thoroughly cleans the surface and removes any excess sand. The casting is now ready for a procedure called fettling, which in turn removes any excess metal from the casting joint-line.

Once the Aga's castings have visited the machine shop, where the necessary holes for fitting have been drilled, they are packed and transported to Ketley to be enamelled. The cast-iron surfaces of every Aga cooker are finished with a vitreous enamel coating, chosen for its durability and colour-retention qualities.

Vitreous enamel is a mixture of

A reputation cast in iron: the modern-day Aga is manufactured in Coalbrookdale and Ketley in the West Midlands using techniques which have remained largely unchanged for eight decades

molten glass, clay and pigment which is bonded on to the cast iron at very high temperatures to form a highly resilient gloss finish. Aga-Rayburn prepares its own enamels at its works in Ketley in Shropshire, probably the largest producer of vitreous enamel in the UK. The entire process takes a week, with every step carried out by hand.

Aga advertising material in the 1990s in particular made much of the hand-built nature of the cooker. One, entitled *Aga: It's a way of life*, told colourfully of the care taken at Coalbrookdale.

Every cooker bearing the famous Aga nameplate is totally hand built. Not for any altruistic reasons, or through sheer stubborn pride, but because, from a purely practical point of view, it's the only way to build an Aga. A unique and superior alternative to mass production.

First of all, what do we mean by hand built? Just that. Every single part of the

finishing and assembly work is performed and repeatedly inspected by human hand and eye.

Enamelling fuses glass on to metal. The shot-blasting process removes all traces of grit from the surface of the cast iron and roughens the surface enough to provide the perfect base for the enamel itself.

A basecoat is sprayed on to the castings, which are then heated in a commercial oven at a temperature of 785°C for 40 minutes. Two further coats of enamel are applied, with the casts being fired between the application of each layer at temperatures which vary according to the chosen colour pigment. Those colours – produced from metal oxides – appear pale and chalky before firing; once fired, however, the high glaze of the vitreous enamel is activated and the enamelling is complete.

Once the enamelling process is finished each Aga undergoes a rigorous checking procedure. Only when this is completed is the Aga

ready to be packed and transported. The end result of such stringent manufacturing processes is that each new Aga produced is unique. In a world where production processes tend to be automated, the Aga stands apart. Each is hand-built by skilled craftsmen, many of them representing the latest in several generations of foundrymen. And, like the human fingerprint, no two Agas are ever exactly the same.

No two, for example, are precisely the same shade. Because of this – and to ensure that, should a customer ever wish to replace any part of the Aga, a true replacement will be available – a colour match is taken and recorded.

In an ever-changing world driven by new technology, the Aga remains a classic, still built today with levels of care befitting its status as a kitchen icon and repaying the vision of the scientist who invented it but never got to see it...

Aga timeline 1869-2002

1869

1901

1909

1912

1922

1929

1931

Nils Gustaf Dalén born in Stenstorp in Skaraborg, a province of Vastergötland in southern Sweden, on November 30, the son of a peasant farmer

Dalén becomes Technical Chief of the Svenska Karbid-och Acetylen A.B. [Swedish Carbide and Acetylene, Ltd.], where he rises to the position of Chief Engineer in 1906.

The firm is reorganised as Svenska Aktiebolaget Gas Accumulator (AGA) [Swedish Gas Accumulator Ltd.] with Dalén himself as Managing Director.

Dalén is blinded in an explosion at a quarry testing site. Later that year he is awarded the Nobel Prize for Physics for his invention of automatic valves for lighthouses. Dalén is unable personally to collect his diploma from the Swedish Royal Academy of Science.

The first Aga is patented by Dalén. The cooker's birth follows months of exhausting experimentation in the kitchen at the inventor's home.

The first Agas are imported to Great Britain by Bell's Asbestos & Engineering Ltd of Slough – 'sole Licensees and Manufacturers for the British Empire (except Canada). Later, a separate company is established to sell the new Agas: Bell's Heat Appliances, later to become part of Allied Ironfounders Ltd, which is established in this year.

The first Aga is sold within the Irish Free State. The cooker is installed by John Masser, owner of A. H. Masser of Dublin.

1933

1935

1936

1937

1941

1947

1948

Faber & Faber publishes *Good Food on the Aga*, written by Ambrose Heath and illustrated by Edward Bawden.

David Ogilvy, Scottish sales representative for Aga, produces his entertaining and informative *The Theory and Practice of Selling an Aga Cooker.*

The New Standard Aga is launched, with a 'guaranteed maximum fuel cost of less than £4 a year'. The model later becomes known as the 47/10 – so called because it cost £47.10s!

Gustaf Dalén, who had been suffering from cancer, dies aged 68.

All existing Aga models, both domestic and heavy duty, are withdrawn and replaced by a range of units with standardised parts. The Aga Standard remains in production until 1972.

Production of the Aga at Smethwick is boosted by the opening of a unit at Ketley, near Telford in Shropshire. Transfer of resources to the export trade during the war leads to a long waiting list for Agas. 'The earliest delivery date for any normal order received must, at the present rate of production, be set at save 27 months ahead.'

W. T. 'Freckles' Wren, Managing Director of Aga Heat Ltd, part of Allied Ironfounders Ltd, announces that more than 50,000 British families now own an Aga.

Aga timeline 1869-2002

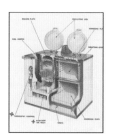

1956   **1961**   **1964**   **1968**   **1969**   **1971**   **1975**

The first colour Agas are introduced: the omnipresent cream vitreous enamel is joined by pale blue, pale green, grey, and white. Black is offered as an optional top-plate colour.

The Aga top plate now comes only in black.

The first oil-fired Aga is launched (Dr Gustaf Dalén had experimented with an oil-fired range in the 1920s). First is the two-oven Model OB, swiftly followed by the larger Model OC and OCB90 with integral water boiler.

A rise in awareness of town gas as a fuel leads to the launch of the first gas-fired Aga. More new colours are unveiled: red, dark blue, dark green, yellow and black.

Glynwed Ltd acquires Allied Ironfounders Ltd and becomes the new owner of the Aga.

Yellow and pale green are withdrawn as Aga colours. Introduction of the OCB135 model.

A further rationalisation of colours by Aga sees the withdrawal of grey, pale blue and black. The first Aga to run on electricity is launched. The EL2 features new styling and is the first Aga not of cast iron. Production ceases after two years.

 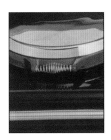  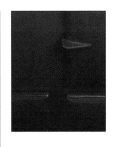    

1978

1985

1987

1991

1992

1995

1996

Black is introduced as a front-plate colour.

The new Electric Aga is launched, a 2-oven Aga in cast iron. It runs on overnight electricity and is vented by a small pipe through the wall

The 4-oven electric Aga arrives.

Jade is unveiled as an additional colour.

More new colour changes are announced: claret and emerald are in; brown is out.

Spring-assisted insulating lids are fitted to all new models; a gold-plating option for chrome fittings is offered; the option of enamelled lids is re-introduced; the script Aga badge is offered as an option; the warming plates on all cookers change from aluminium to hard anodised; the hot cupboard top plates now overlap the cooker itself.

January sees the launch of Aga's first conventional cooker – the Electric Module. September sees the introduction of British Racing Green and pewter and consolidation of the dark green option as Hunter Green. Red and emerald are withdrawn; second notice of withdrawal of brown. In October, the Aga Companion is launched.

Aga timeline 1869-2002

1997

1998

1999

2000

2001

2002

Golden yellow and royal blue are introduced, making a grand total of 13 colours in the standard Aga range and five in the Select range. The metal used for construction of the hot cupboard is changed to aludip steel and mild steel base plate. An electric hotplate option for the 4-oven Aga is introduced.

A gas hotplate option is offered for both the Module and the Companion. Red is deleted from the Select colour range.

David Ogilvy, dies in France. In March the Masterchef is unveiled to Aga distributors.

The Aga Foodservice Group is created with a reorganisation of the businesses within Glynwed International plc. The Masterchef comes on to the market.

January: a gas hob option is made available for all four-oven Agas. February: flagship store in Knightsbridge opens; launch of Agalinks.com – an internet service for Aga owners and non-owners alike. September: launch of the Iron Age marketing initiative. Acquisition of CookCraft, Fired Earth and Elgin & Hall. Launch of Aga Classic and Aga 2000 special edition models.

The Six-Four Series is unveiled, as well as the Omnia range of cookware. March: AFG acquires Boston-based home fashions company Domain. The Aga refrigerator and freezer come to market; the five-oven Aga – dubbed the 'ultimate Aga' – is slated for launch.

Index

Index

Index

Photography and illustration

The vision of a genius

All pictures courtesy of the AGA archives, Sweden,
except: Dalén's sleep-prolonger, p17, from *Svenska*
by Uppleva Uttrycka; Albert Einstein, p25, © Royal
Photographic Society / Jarche and courtesy of Retna
Images Limited; Dalén's family and maid, p28,
© Midland Independent Magazines

The Aga arrives in Britain

All pictures courtesy of the Aga Foodservice Group
archives, UK, except: Brentford plant, p37, courtesy
AGA Sweden; 1930 Bestobell staff,
courtesy Richard Bedwell; Thomas Grattan Bedwell,
p44, courtesy of Richard Bedwell

The Aga goes to war

All pictures courtesy of the the Aga Foodservice Group
archives, UK, except Philip Garrod, p77, by the author

Rise of the Agastocracy

All pictures courtesy of the the Aga Foodservice Group
archives, UK, except: *The Archers*, p86, © BBC

Television; Coronation cartoon, p103, originally
published in *Punch*

Aga chameleon

All pictures courtesy of the the Aga Foodservice Group
archives, UK, except: p60 © Hulton Archive

Electrifying times

All pictures courtesy of the the Aga Foodservice Group
archives, UK, except: Max Wall, p124, courtesy of
Pauline Torode; Aga salesman, p125, courtesy of
Richard Sizer; Pam Ayers, p126, © Midland Independent
Magazines

Conspicuous consumption

All pictures courtesy of the Aga Foodservice Group
archives, UK, except: Jilly Cooper, p141, © Craig
Holmes; Alan Bishop, p146, by the author; Foundry
workers, p150, © *Shropshire Star*

Are you living comfortably?

All pictures courtesy of the the Aga Foodservice Group

archives, UK, except: Simon Page, p162, by the author;
Mary Berry, p163, courtesy Mary Berry

Back to the future

All pictures courtesy of the the Aga Foodservice Group
archives, UK, except: Agalinks images, p177, courtesy of
Morris Nicholson Cartwright Ltd; Richard Scarre, p178,
courtesy of AFG; Laura James, p178, © Craig Holmes;
Jamie Oliver, p187 & 190, © Craig Holmes; William
McGrath, p196, © Midland Independent Magazines

History in the making

All pictures courtesy of the the Aga Foodservice Group
archives, UK, except: modern manufacturing images,
pp198-207, © Rob Hadley; Don Flack, p201, by the
author

Acknowledgments

A book such as this – the collective thoughts, memories and opinions of so many people – is made by the quality of that involvement. I have been so fortunate. That the Aga was unique I was in no doubt; that it was regarded with such fondness I had little idea and I have been touched by the generosity shown by so many. My concern now is that, in offering my thanks to those who have shared their thoughts, my memory – addled by middle-age – will let me down. But here goes…

Firstly, a big thank you to all at Aga, particularly to Simon Page and Richard Scarre for their unstinting support and guidance. They were there for me to lean on from the point when this book was nothing more than an idea scribbled on the back of a cigarette packet. To Alan Bishop, Arthur Price and Don Flack – Aga stalwarts all of them – for giving up so much of their time and expertise. To William McGrath for allowing me to root around the Aga archives with such unrestricted access and for his enthusiasm for this project. And to Dawn Roads for remaining cheerful in the face of innumerable requests for pictures and information.

I owe a huge debt of gratitude to those who allowed me such a personal insight into their lives. They include Swedish historian Ebbe Almqvist, Gustaf Silverstolpe and other members of Dr Dalén's family, Hazel Jordan, Richard and Prue Bedwell, Philip and Neil Garrod and Iain Gillespie. I would also like to single out an unsung hero of this book: Pam Vernon-Roberts, who loaned me so many of her vintage Aga advertisements.

My thanks to Jilly Cooper, who always shows such great kindness to fellow writers, to Jamie Oliver for taking time out of his hectic schedule, and to Mary Berry for talking so lyrically about her Aga years.

Thank you, too, to all those (too many, sadly, to list here) who responded to my appeals for information on the Aga's 80 years.

Finally, my thanks to Jon Croft, who started out as my publisher and became a friend, and to Matt and Meg and everyone else at Absolute Press for their invaluable help in turning this book into a reality.

Tim James
2002

THE
AGA
REGD. TRADE MARK
COOKER

has a guaranteed _maximum_ fuel consumption of less than

£5

A YEAR

burning continuously

Follow this guide to the
AGA COOKER Showrooms
(Regd. Trade Mark)

20, NORTH AUDLEY ST.
LONDON, W.1

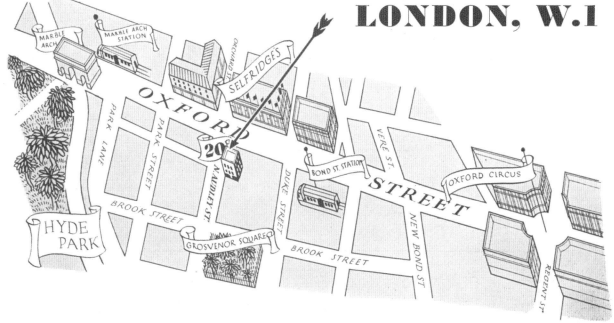